I0833331

Motivational Stories for Extraordinary Boys

Empowering Journeys of Bravery, Growth, and Boundless Possibilities to Inspire the Next Generation of Young Men

Table of Contents

Introduction

This lovely book is not merely a collection of the most motivational and inspirational stories of people like you, who defied the odds, made their dreams real, and inspired millions with their work. It's much more than that. Think of it like a compass directing you to find your true North - your purpose - and how to follow your heart until you reach your destination.

Every page shows you the secret recipe to success and teaches you how to turn the obstacles blocking your path into stepping stones. When you have read this book, you'll feel like a hero because you'll know you have what it takes to go after your goals and crush them.

How is this book different from others? For one, the stories here are of people from many walks of life. You'll learn about heroes in sports, arts, science, politics, and more. The stories have been carefully chosen, so you'll find something you can relate to. They've been written to act as a mirror, reflecting the sides of yourself you had no idea you've always had within you. They're a road map, showing you how to become someone who never quits, even when people give you a laundry list of reasons to give up on your dreams.

You see, these tenacious go-getters didn't do what they did because there's some rule book telling you how to handle disappointment, be brave, and keep saying yes to yourself when everyone else is screaming no at you. Their mindset inspired every action they took and every choice they made. They acted as they did because they truly believed in themselves and what they stood for.

So, with this book, you'll pull back the curtains and peek in on some of the most brilliant minds ever to see how they think. You'll find excellent quotes from each inspirational person, giving clues on how to succeed like they have. This way, you'll know what happened in the world around them and also within them.

Are you prepared to be awed by how much strength you have within? Are you ready to learn how people like you achieved their greatness? Then, all you need to do is dive into the first chapter and begin your inspiring odyssey.

Be warned: You'll never be the same once you've read this book - but that's a good thing because it means you'll know your worth and the power inside you to change your life and the world for good.

Chapter 1: Those Who Dared to Dream

Do you know what it means to be a visionary? It means you see past the way things are. You see the possibilities. When others are stuck in the past, blaming themselves or others for how things are, you focus on what could be better. Others may think your ideas are silly or impossible, but as a visionary, you aren't afraid to take action and see what works. In this chapter, you'll learn about three renowned visionaries who changed the world because they weren't afraid to dream big.

Martin Luther King Jr.

Once upon a time, far too many people judged others based on the color of their skin. Black Americans were treated as if they weren't human. If you were African American in those days, it meant you'd have to sit in your designated area so White people wouldn't feel "uncomfortable" or be "offended" by your presence. That's only one way you would have been judged and discriminated against. It was a terrible time, and racism was an ugly problem Martin Luther King Jr. was determined to fix.

Martin Luther King Jr.
Mike Licht, ATTRIBUTION 2.0 GENERIC, CC BY 2.0
<https://creativecommons.org/licenses/by/2.0/>
https://www.flickr.com/photos/notionscapital/5360731135

Martin was born in 1929 and witnessed segregation (separating them out from other races) and discrimination (treating them differently from other races) against Black people. He saw firsthand how the system was set up against Black people. He saw the many ways the racists treated his fellow Black people, and this ignited a fire in his heart that burned hot and bright, fueled by the desire to end the cruel and heartless treatment of Black people.

Martin wanted his people to be free and everyone to be treated equally, no matter their appearance. He was right to have this dream. Can you imagine walking around and seeing signs that read "Blacks Only" and "Whites Only?" It was an unjust way to be treated.

Fortunately, Martin was part of a loving family. His father was a minister, and Martin looked up to him. His father taught him always to speak the truth and stand up for what's right, no matter how loudly people try to shut him down.

So, Martin chose to walk in his father's footsteps by becoming a Baptist church minister. He had a strong belief that the only way to stop the horrible treatment of Black people was to be loving and seek justice. Mahatma Gandhi's teachings inspired him. When India struggled to become independent, Gandhi spoke up and stood up for its rights by choosing nonviolent protests. Martin thought he could pull off this, too.

Martin Luther King Junior was not someone who believed in retaliation. There was no way he was going to repay the oppressors of Black people with their own coin. Instead, he believed he could achieve equality peacefully as Gandhi did. So, how did he do this? He organized his people to go on peaceful marches.

The good minister and political philosopher got African American people to boycott any interests or businesses that weren't in favor of equality. The entire time, he wasn't riling the people up. Instead, he kept telling them to remain calm no matter what. He encouraged them to always respect others, even when angry or hostile about being oppressed. Have you ever been in a situation where someone keeps pressing your buttons, and you try your best to remain calm? Then, you know this was not an easy thing to do. But Martin Luther King somehow inspired everyone to keep a cool head.

Even when racists were using horrible language and being violent toward Black people, these courageous, resilient African Americans remained calm. Did they lose their cool when they were being beaten? No. Water cannons were launched at them, and some were arrested. Yet, inspired by Martin, they chose to remain nonviolent.

You see, Martin didn't allow the pushback he received to stop him from going after his goal. He dreamed of equality and knew that if he persevered, he would have it. He realized that if he responded to violence with anger, he'd never accomplish his goals.

In 1963, there was a landmark event. Two hundred and fifty thousand people in Washington, DC, prepared for the March on Washington. They wanted better-paying jobs and freedom. Martin Luther King gave the iconic "I Have a Dream" speech on the steps of the Lincoln Memorial. It was, and still is, one of the most powerful speeches in history.

Can you imagine what it feels like to stand in front of a quarter of a million people? Can you think what it's like to know that each person is full of hope for a better future because of you? It was a lot of pressure for Martin to bear, but he carried it gracefully. He'd come so far and wasn't about to give up.

One of the beautiful things about Martin Luther King's speech to the people is he never called for violence. He could have talked about being angry, but he didn't. He could have encouraged Black people to retaliate. If it were someone else, they'd probably call for revenge. But he didn't. Instead, he chose to talk about how he saw the future.

Martin painted a beautiful picture of what he thought was possible. He shared his vision with his people, discussing a time when everyone would be treated equally regardless of appearance. Martin reminded everyone that America was supposed to be the land of the free.

When Martin delivered his speech that day, many Americans were motivated to join the fight against inequality and injustice against Black people. He proved that violence isn't always the answer. He moved many hearts with his words alone. The greatest lesson you could learn from Martin's story is you can fight for what you believe in without violence.

Unfortunately, Martin died in 1968, but thankfully, his dream continued to live. If he weren't as bold and courageous as he was in starting the movement for equality, Black people wouldn't be where they are today in America. Segregation is now illegal. Now, everyone has a say in politics because they have the right to vote, no matter where they're from or their skin color.

Does this mean that the battle for equality is over? Not quite. There are still a few traces of racism, inequality, and injustice toward people of color. But thanks to Martin's work, it's only a matter of time before this oppressive and unfair system ends.

Martin's inspirational story shows that even when things appear impossible and people say, "Things will never change because they've always been that way," you can cause the change you want to see. If you put your mind to it, speak up, and work passionately to get what you want.

So, if you have a dream, you should give it everything. Always stand up for it no matter what, and refuse to give up. You will face some challenges and difficulties on your way, but know that if you keep a positive attitude and a resilient spirit, you will succeed.

Famous Quotes

1. *Darkness cannot drive out darkness. Only light can do that. Hate cannot drive out hate. Only love can do that.*
2. *The time is always right to do what is right.*
3. *Our lives begin to end the day we become silent about things that matter.*
4. *Faith is taking the first step even when you don't see the whole staircase.*
5. *Let no man pull you so low as to hate him.*

Marie Curie

Marie Sklodowska Curie was born in Poland in 1867. That sure does feel like a long time ago, but it doesn't make her accomplishments any less remarkable today. Marie lived in Warsaw, and at the time, it was rare to find other little girls like her who shared the same interests. Most girls loved to play with dolls, but not Marie. She was more interested in numbers and how life works.

Marie Curie. Source:
https://commons.wikimedia.org/wiki/File:Mariecurie.jpg

Marie was the youngest of five children. Her parents were school teachers who didn't make a lot of money. Sadly, Marie's mother died, and her father couldn't afford to take care of her. But Marie was not someone you could keep down. She decided to do something about her situation. She became a governess. Whenever she had free time, she read as much as possible. When she wasn't at work, she researched and studied many things.

As much as Marie would have loved to become a teacher, there was one problem. She didn't have enough money to continue studying. This was sad because, at the time, if you were a woman and wanted to be independent, you had to become a teacher. Fortunately for Marie, her sister invited her to Paris to attend university. As you can imagine, Marie was beyond ecstatic.

So, in 1891, she packed her bags and moved to France. Marie enrolled in the Sorbonne University in Paris as soon as she arrived in France. It was a dream come true for her. Finally, she'd get the chance to study mathematics and physics to her heart's content.

While at university, she met Pierre Curie. Pierre was a scientist, much like Marie, and eventually, they fell in love and married in 1895. Her birth name was Maria. But once she married Pierre, she spelled her name like the French did, with an E at the end instead of an A.

Marie and her husband worked hard at the School of Chemistry and Physics in Paris. They were studying uranium because they noticed it gives off invisible rays, which they thought could be useful. They knew about these rays thanks to Professor Henri Becquerel's work, which showed that they could move through fog, film, and solid matter, allowing electricity to pass through them.

Marie Curie made several discoveries of her own. For instance, she found that a unique mineral known as pitchblende had uranium ore, and its radioactivity level was much higher than that of uranium. She realized she only got such dramatic measurements because something other than the uranium caused those results.

As great as Marie's discovery was, there was an issue. It was difficult for her to prove her theories because the uranium's radioactive material was too tiny to be detected. She knew in her heart that she'd discovered a new element, even if her colleagues doubted her.

Choosing not to be discouraged by her doubters and naysayers, Marie worked hard to discover this new element. Pierre helped with her research. Together, they tried numerous things, from grinding the pitchblende to dissolving it in acid and separating all the elements they could find. With time, they found a black powder within the pitchblende, which seemed to cause the radioactivity. They called this powder polonium.

Finally, Marie found the new element others said didn't exist. She noticed something interesting because of her research. The remaining liquid was also high in radioactivity even after the polonium was extracted. Marie knew there was another element to be discovered, one even more radioactive than polonium, but in even smaller amounts. She and her husband named this element radium, even if they didn't yet have a pure sample.

Working with an Austrian factory, Marie extracted the uranium from pitchblende. She spent a lot of money buying the waste product from processing it. Everyone thought it was worthless, but Marie didn't let other people's opinions stop her. The waste product from the uranium was more radioactive than pitchblende and, thankfully, cheaper, too. It meant Marie could get as much as she needed to study the material properly.

Sadly, she and her husband didn't realize their work made them sick. Each day, they felt more tired than the last. They'd chalked it up to working long and hard, but really, they were experiencing the start of radiation sickness. No one had experienced this sickness before, so the scientific couple wouldn't have known to stop what they were doing or take better safety precautions. They worked with their bare hands, which were always inflamed and raw.

Eventually, Marie would find what she was looking for in 1902. She discovered radium chloride. As it turns out, radium is used in treating cancer, which is a horrible disease. Her work has saved many lives.

Marie and Pierre won the Nobel Prize for Physics in 1903 for their discoveries in radioactivity. Marie was the first woman to win the Nobel Prize. She also passed her physics doctorate thesis in the same year. Three years later, she lost Pierre in an accident when a horse and a cart knocked him down.

Being a courageous, resilient person, Marie found a way to push through her sadness. She took Pierre's former position as a professor at the Sorbonne. From then on, she achieved much more, leading her to win another Nobel Prize 8 years after her first, in 1911. This new prize was for developing a way to measure radioactivity.

There aren't many as determined as Marie was, constantly creating new inventions and innovations. Some people do one thing and think they can't do more, but not Marie. She always kept the ball rolling. Thanks to her inventive mind, she devised the idea for an X-ray unit. This invention would help medical personnel find wounded soldiers' injuries. Since the unit was portable, it could be carried as close to the battlefront as needed.

In October 1914, the first of her machines were ready. They were called Petites Curies, French for "little Curies." Now, she could have stopped there. She could have let the doctors and others in the medical field handle things themselves, but she didn't. Marie went right to the war front.

Working with her 17-year-old daughter, Irene, Marie used her little Curies to X-ray the wounded soldiers and find the shrapnel, bullets, and fractures lodged in their bodies so the surgeons could remove them and save their lives.

The war ended, but that didn't mean Marie's work was done. She continued researching things that interested her, kept teaching, and worked as the head of a laboratory. She did so well that she was offered even more awards recognizing her brilliant achievements.

In 1921, Marie Curie was awarded the Ellan Richards Research Prize. In 1923, the Grand Prix du Marquis d'Argenteuil, and in 1931, she received Edinburgh University's Cameron Prize. She passed away in 1934 but lives on through her discoveries and inspirational stories.

What can you learn from Marie Curie's story? When you want something, keep going, even if no one believes in you. You must believe in yourself and trust your intuition. Eventually, your perseverance will pay off. Also, be curious. Ask questions, and when you get answers, ask more questions. Your curiosity will lead you to marvelous discoveries.

Famous Quotes

1. *Nothing in life is to be feared. It is only to be understood. Now is the time to understand more so that we may fear less.*
2. *Life is not easy for any of us. But what of that? We must have perseverance and, above all, confidence in ourselves. We must believe that we are gifted with something and that this thing, at whatever cost, must be attained.*

3. *A scientist in his laboratory is not a mere technician. He is also a child confronting natural phenomena that impress him as though they were fairy tales.*
4. *I was taught that the way of progress was neither swift nor easy.*
5. *I am among those who think that science has great beauty.*

Steve Jobs

You can't talk about technology without mentioning Steve Jobs. He was born in 1955 in San Francisco, California. Steve was adopted by Paul and Clara Jobs shortly after he was born. Since he was a child, Steve's heart would light up at anything related to gadgets or electronics. Fortunately, his dad encouraged him. This young genius learned a lot from Paul, like how to open up electronics and put them back together.

Steve Jobs.

Matthew Yohe, CC BY-SA 3.0 <https://creativecommons.org/licenses/by-sa/3.0>, via Wikimedia Commons https://commons.wikimedia.org/wiki/File:Steve_Jobs_Headshot_2010-CROP_(cropped_2).jpg

Steve attended Homestead High School in Cupertino, California, and then to Portland's Reed College in 1972. You'd think Steve was so good at what he did because he paid close attention in school, right? Well, he dropped out after half a year. He stopped attending Reed College because he wanted to save his parents money.

Steve didn't quit his auditing classes, though. At night, his friends let him sleep on their floors. When he needed to eat, he'd pick up Coke bottles and return them for food money. A Hare Krishna temple was nearby, and Steve would go there to eat since they offered free meals once a week.

Steve wanted to find spiritual enlightenment. He wanted to know his purpose. He felt strongly that the only way was to go to India. His choice may not seem logical, but that's the thing about following your gut. It won't always make sense, but it will lead you to the best places in life.

So, in 1974, Steve took a trip to India. He also became a student of Zen Buddhism. When he returned to California after his spiritual quest, he and Steve Wozniak attended meetings held by the Homebrew Computer Club. In 1976, they partnered to create Apple Computer, Inc., which had its headquarters in the garage of Jobs's home.

They worked hard and eventually created their first product in 1977, the Apple I. This device was their first "baby," and they built it by hand. The following year, they developed the Apple II; for the next ten years, this would be the product everyone wanted. It would seem Steve had finally found his calling, and he'd struck gold.

Things didn't remain smooth for too long, though. In 1985, the board members of Apple were battling Steve because they wanted full control of the company. In the end, he had to leave the company. But he didn't let this get him down. Instead, he launched another company called NeXT Inc. NeXT served higher education institutions and businesses by developing computer platforms.

A year later, Steve took over Lucasfilm's computer graphics division, The Graphics Group, which was later called Pixar. This company created Toy Story, an animated movie that became a massive hit and won hearts worldwide.

Apple saw Steve was doing much better than they thought he would with his NeXT company. They made him an offer of $429 million, which he accepted. The deal was completed in February 1997. Not only did he pocket a nice chunk of change, but he was also reinstated at Apple. In September 1997, he took over as interim CEO.

While Steve was at Apple for the second time, he developed a new line of amazing products and software that secured Apple's place as the tech giant it is today - the iMac, iTunes, iPod, iPhone, and iPad. Each product was a massive hit with tech lovers. Before Steve returned to the company he built by hand with his friend and namesake, Apple was losing money. His return caused Apple's profits to soar beyond anything the board had thought possible.

Sadly, Steve Jobs had been dealing with pancreatic cancer for a long time. He lost that battle in 2011 when he passed away. It was a dark day in the world of technology. One of the world's most brilliant and inventive minds was gone for good.

Steve Jobs left behind a legacy that will last for a lifetime, not only in technology but also in other business and life aspects. What can you learn from him? Passion is important. You'll go a long way if you choose the work that aligns with your passions.

Also, like Steve, don't be afraid to step outside the box. Instead of thinking of what's already been done, open your mind. Think of what could be that doesn't exist yet, and realize you could be the one to make it happen. This is the power of vision. This is what it means to be a visionary.

Famous Quotes

1. *The people who are crazy enough to think they can change the world are the ones who do.*
2. *Your work is going to fill a large part of your life, and the only way to be truly satisfied is to do what you believe is great work. And the only way to do great work is to love what you do. If you haven't found it yet, keep looking. Don't settle. As with all matters of the heart, you'll know when you find it.*
3. *Remembering that you are going to die is the best way I know to avoid the trap of thinking you have something to lose. You are already naked. There is no reason not to follow your heart.*
4. *Quality is more important than quantity. One home run is much better than two doubles.*
5. *For the past 33 years, I have looked in the mirror every morning and asked myself: "If today were the last day of my life, would I want to do what I am about to do today?" And whenever the answer has been "No" for too many days in a row, I know I need to change something.*

Chapter 2: Incredible Bravery

Sometimes, you are terrified to do things you know you must. But did you know being afraid doesn't mean you shouldn't act? Fear is a sign that you should keep going. Sometimes, that scared feeling means you're on the right path. So, the next time fear stops you from chasing your desires, remind yourself it is only an emotion, and your emotions don't have to be your boss. You're in charge.

Being courageous isn't without fear. When you have courage, it means even though you're afraid, you'll keep going because you know what you're doing is right in your heart. When you're brave, you look fear in the eyes, know it can't hurt you, and set it aside to focus on your passion. Here are stories of courageous, brave people to inspire you to be like them when the time comes to stand up for what's right.

Malala Yousafzai

Malala Yousafzai was born in 1997 in Pakistan. Specifically, she was born in the Khyber Pakhtunkhwa Province in the Swat Valley to her parents, Ziauddin and Tor Pekai Yousafzai. She has two younger brothers. Malala's dad deeply loved education and believed everyone deserved access to it. Since he was in charge of one of the city's learning institutions, schooling was essential to the Yousafzai family. When Malala was little, she took after her dad. She wanted to learn and know as much as possible. She'd slip into classes and make believe she was teaching her students.

Malala Yousafzai.

DFID - UK Department for International Development, CC BY 2.0 <https://creativecommons.org/licenses/by/2.0>, via Wikimedia Commons https://commons.wikimedia.org/wiki/File:Malala_Yousafzai_2015.jpg

Life became a nightmare for Malala, her family, and the people in Swat Valley when she was only ten years old. In 2007, the Taliban terrorists occupied their homeland. They wanted control and didn't stop at politics. They bullied people into how they socialized with one another.

The Taliban menace spread too far, too fast. They took over the northwestern region of Pakistan. Even in this modern world, this problematic group believes girls have no business being in school. They banned every girl from getting an education. They banned watching television. They even banned dancing. You could say these terrorists put the "*ban*" in *Taliban.*

Of all the horrible things they wanted, nothing was more important to the Taliban than keeping girls out of school. By the end of 2008, this destructive group had not only terrorized the beautiful people of Pakistan mercilessly with their suicide attacks but also destroyed at least 400 schools.

Can you imagine living under the rule of such horrible people? That must be nothing short of terrifying. Yet, Malala didn't change her mind about getting an education. She believed she and everyone else had the right to go to school. So, she stood up to Pakistan's bullies, even when afraid.

Malala and her father dared to raise their voices against the Taliban. They spoke up against their cruelty and ridiculous beliefs about education being a bad thing. Once, on Pakistani TV, Malala asked, "How dare the Taliban take away my basic right to education?" That's right. She had the guts to say that on live TV, knowing how violent, vicious, and vindictive these terrorists are.

Malala was a courageous girl who was not about to be silenced, even though she knew the Taliban could end her life for speaking against their evil deeds. Early in 2009, she found a way to get her message out by blogging anonymously for the British Broadcasting Corporation (BBC). She wrote for the Urdu language version of the site, sharing everything about what life with the Taliban rule was like in the Swat Valley and expressing how much she'd love to return to school.

Since Malala couldn't write her real name on her blog posts (that would have made it easy for the Taliban to find and silence her), she used the name "Gul Makai" on the site. She wrote about what it's like to be forced to remain at home rather than go to school. She expressed her thoughts about what the terrorists hoped to accomplish by keeping girls and women from education.

When Malala wrote her first piece on the BBC site, she was only 11 years old. She was proof that courage isn't something only adults can have. You can have it, too. You may think her superpower is that she has no fear, but that's not it. One entry Malala wrote on her BBC blog was titled "I Am Afraid." She spoke up even though she felt fear in her little heart.

In "I Am Afraid," Malala shared her fears with the world. She was afraid that with how the Taliban oppressed people, it would only be a matter of time before war broke out and destroyed her lovely homeland, the Swat Valley. Pakistan was going to war with the Taliban. It wasn't a matter of if they would, but when they would.

On May 5, 2009, the worst of Malala's fears came to pass. She and many others were forced to abandon their home. They became internally displaced people (IDPs), as they had to find a safe haven that was miles away from where they once knew and loved as home.

After a few weeks away from Swat Valley, Malala picked up where she had left off, sharing her thoughts through the media. Her voice grew even louder as she spoke up for the right to attend school. Clearly, she had no intention of staying quiet for anyone's comfort.

Malala drew the attention of Pakistanis, and many looked to her and her father as defenders of the right to free, quality education. As a result of her activism, in 2011, she was nominated for the International Children's Peace Prize. She received the National Youth Peace Prize award in Pakistan the same year. This was something worth celebrating for most people, but not everyone was happy about it.

Malala's voice had grown loud enough for the Taliban. They didn't like what she had to say one bit. So, when she was 15 years old, they attempted to assassinate her. Imagine a group of grown men so terrified of a young 15-year-old that they wanted to kill her. That's what a coward looks like.

On the morning of October 9, 2012, the Taliban shot Malala Yousafzai. Thankfully, she didn't die. If the Taliban could go back in time and undo what they did, they probably would. Why? The outpouring of support and love for Malala Yousafzai worldwide put the Taliban's shameful actions and horrendously dangerous ideas in the international limelight. According to Deutsche Welle, a German public state broadcaster, Malala had become "the most famous teenager in the world."

When Malala recovered from the gunshot wound, she became even more of an activist. She kept fighting for girls' right to go to school, setting up a non-profit organization called the Malala Fund. She wrote her book, "I Am Malala," with British author and journalist Christina Lamb.

Malala's book became an international bestseller for a good reason. Everyone wanted to know the story of the girl brave enough to speak up against men with guns. Everyone wanted to know how her fiery passion for free, quality education for all couldn't be stopped, even by a bullet. Her story reflected the experiences of the many Pakistani girls and young women who couldn't speak out because of the Taliban's tyranny.

In 2014, Malala received the Nobel Peace Prize with India's Kailash Satyarthi for advocating for children's rights. She was only 17 and the youngest person ever to win the Nobel Prize laureate.

Winning a prize wasn't enough for Malala. She wanted to see genuine change. So, even now, she keeps advocating for education. She stokes the fires of courage and bravery in young girls, encouraging them to be the change they wish to see as she has. Millions of people globally have been touched by Malala's fighting spirit. Undoubtedly, her story has also touched you. She is the global symbol of peaceful, vocal protest.

Famous Quotes

1. *Let us make our future now, and let us make our dreams tomorrow's reality.*
2. *One child, one teacher, one pen, and one book can change the world.*
3. *Some people only ask others to do something. I believe that why should I wait for someone else? Why don't I take a step and move forward?*
4. *When the world is silent, even one voice becomes powerful.*
5. *I truly believe the only way we can create global peace is through not only educating our minds but our hearts and our souls.*

Nelson Mandela

During a period in South Africa, racism was even more extreme than it is now. The political system, called apartheid, separated people into "Whites" and "nonWhites." Imagine what it's like to believe your skin color, which you can't control, makes you better than others. Those who believe this think they should get special, better treatment because of how much or little melanin they have.

Nelson Mandela.

South Africa The Good News / www.sagoodnews.co.za, CC BY 2.0 <https://creativecommons.org/licenses/by/2.0>, via Wikimedia Commons https://commons.wikimedia.org/wiki/File:Nelson_Mandela-2008_(edit)_(cropped).jpg

This apartheid system wasn't only racist. It was dangerous. It gave the "Whites" in South Africa the legal right to oppress others who didn't look like them. It was a terrible time, and the world was a bleak one to live in. It seemed like the horrors would never end.

No one knew that when Nelson Rolihlahla Mandela was born, he would become one of the prominent critics of apartheid in South Africa. He was born in Mvezo, a little village in South Africa's Eastern Cape, in 1918, and of the Tembu Madiba clan who speak Xhosa. His father was a local chief and the monarch's counselor.

Mandela went to a local mission school and the University of Fort Hare, where Black Africans could get quality education. He was expelled for participating in a protest against the University's policies.

Mandela moved to Johannesburg in 1943. There, he became a member of the African National Congress or ANC, a political party strongly against racial segregation in South Africa. It didn't take him long to move through the ranks. He also helped form the ANC Youth League to get more young people interested in the movement.

Nine years after Mandela's move to Jo'burg (as South Africans fondly call Johannesburg), he and others with the same passion for abolishing apartheid united to create the Defiance Campaign. This campaign was formed to make big moves against apartheid laws. In the same year, 1952, Mandela formed the first-ever Black law firm in the country with Oliver Tambo. This law firm was dedicated to offering legal counsel to people affected by unfair apartheid rules at a fraction of the cost or free.

For a while, it seemed like the peaceful protests weren't changing anything. The South African government was arrogant and continued enforcing laws that discriminated against people based on race. So, along with the ANC, Mandela called for armed resistance.

It was clear to Mandela that the only language the South African government understood was violence, and those in the movement had to protect themselves somehow. So, in 1961, Mandela was among the people who founded Umkhonto we Sizwe, which means "Spear of the Nation." This was the armed extension of the ANC.

The following year, Mandela was arrested. He was accused of inciting the South African people to violence and for not using a passport when he left the country. It's funny how tyrants, terrorists, and other terrible people don't realize when they do something that leads to their downfall - and that's a good thing.

When Mandela stood on trial for his "crimes," the authorities expected him to testify in his defense, but he didn't. Instead, he turned the trial into an opportunity. He gave a powerful, rousing speech. This speech made every "nonwhite" South African and ally against apartheid more determined to end the oppressive political system. Mandela famously said, "I have cherished the ideal of a democratic and free society. It is an ideal for which I am prepared to die." His courage was like nothing anyone had seen before.

Mandela received a five-year prison sentence. He was on trial again in 1964. This time, he'd been accused of sabotage. This trial was called the Rivonia Trial. In the dock, he gave another powerful statement. This time, he spoke about why the ANC needed to switch from nonviolent protest to using arms to protect the anti-apartheid movement and the people who kept it going. Of course, he was found guilty. This time, he received a life sentence on Robben Island.

For the next 18 years, Mandela was in prison. It seemed as if all hope was lost, but he kept going, even though the prison's conditions were harsh. He continued his advocacy from behind bars, calling for apartheid to end. While in prison, he educated himself and got a Bachelor of Laws degree, thanks to a correspondence program by the University of London.

Mandela moved from Robben Island to Pollsmoor Prison on the mainland in 1982. Six years later, he was moved to a minimum-security prison and placed under house arrest.

The entire time Mandela was in prison, the South African government was feeling the heat. The pressure on them was increasing, which was good for the country. Many called for the end of apartheid. It became obvious to the ruling "Whites" that their time was up. If they didn't give up their power, it was only a matter of time before the people took it from them by any means necessary, even at the cost of their lives.

The oppressed South African people had had enough. They were prepared to sacrifice everything rather than spend another day letting the tyrants in their government treat them as less than human. The government finally yielded. In 1990, a new president was elected. His name was Frederik Willem de Klerk. He turned against his party's wishes. He unbanned the ANC and ordered Mandela's immediate release.

Now out of prison, it was Mandela who handled the ANC's negotiations with the new president to stop apartheid once and for all. Thanks to these negotiations, South Africa finally experienced its first elections in which all races could participate in 1994. Nelson Mandela would become South Africa's first Black president.

Becoming the first Black ruler of a nation that had suffered under the tyranny of rulers from the "white" minority was a landmark event. Still, it didn't mean Mandela's work was done. He had to put out the fires of apartheid that still burned. Not everyone was happy about everyone having the basic human right to live with dignity, regardless of skin color.

Mandela had to work on erasing the tension between races and creating a new constitution that was fair to everyone. He set up a Truth and Reconciliation Commission to investigate past cases where human rights were abused resulting from apartheid. He and his government faced many challenges, yet they made much progress. Formerly oppressed Black, Asian, and Colored (mixed race) people had better living conditions, access to quality health care and education, and the chance to prosper financially at long last.

By 1999, Mandela had stepped down as South Africa's president but had never stopped fighting for human rights until he passed away in 2013. He was the picture of bravery and courage. He believed in his vision of a just and fair world where everyone's treated equally. His work has left a lasting impact on South Africans and the world.

Famous Quotes

1. *Do not judge me by my successes. Judge me by how many times I fell down and got back up again.*
2. *It always seems impossible until it's done.*
3. *Lead from the back - and let others believe they are in front.*
4. *There is no passion to be found in playing small - in settling for a life that is less than the one you are capable of living.*
5. *As I have said, the first thing is to be honest with yourself. You can never have an impact on society if you have not changed yourself.*

Harriet Tubman

Born Araminta Ross, Harriet Tubman was born in 1822 in Dorchester County, Maryland. She was born into tough times, as slavery wasn't abolished back then. An overseer of the enslaved people had inflicted a head injury on Araminta by throwing a heavy metal weight. They'd meant to hit a different person (not that it's okay to hit people), but they hit Araminta instead. Due to this incident, she had to deal with pain, dizzy spells, and hypersomnia (she slept a lot). She battled with these struggles for the rest of her life.

Harriet Tubman.

https://commons.wikimedia.org/wiki/File:Harriet_Tubman_1895.jpg

When Araminta was 22, she married John Tubman. He was Black and free. After marriage, she ditched the name Araminta Ross to Harriet Tubman. Five years later, in 1849, her life was about to be shaken up.

Harriet overheard overseers discussing selling her to a different person. She wasn't about to have them send her to a place where things could be worse, and she was tired of living life as less than human. This conversation made her realize she was going to take back her freedom. She decided to escape. There was no other option. But her husband didn't want to leave, so she made the tough decision to leave him behind and journey to Philadelphia (Philly).

Fortunately, Harriet's escape plan worked. In Philly, she found work and saved money. The year after she arrived in Philly, she went back to Maryland to set her sister and two children free from their oppressors' tyranny.

Harriet didn't know it then, but she'd found her purpose as a conductor who helped enslaved African Americans find their freedom. She used a network of safe houses and secret routes called the Underground Railroad. She had become a conductor.

For the next ten years, Harriet played her part in 13 dangerous missions to save 70 enslaved Black people. Her family and friends were of those she rescued. How did she pull it off? Harriet worked on creating a network of people willing to help her. These people were "stationmasters." Their job was to safely stash the escapees in safe houses and barns along their journey.

Harriet knew Maryland like the back of her hand. She learned it was best to travel by tracking the North Star. She also knew which authorities were happy to take a bribe to allow escapees to pass freely.

Harriet was brilliant, especially in gathering the intelligence for a successful mission. She developed a communication system to tell people when it was safe to come out and when they had to abandon their plan. The people who depended on her knew what she told them, whether by making owl sounds, singing specific songs, or other means.

This hero learned it was best to attempt her rescue missions during winter since the nights would be longer and easier to cover her tracks. She gave it substantial thought and concluded that Saturdays were the best days to escape since runaways could not be reported in the newspaper until Mondays.

Sometimes, Harriet would dress up as a man, an older woman, or a free, middle-class Black woman. She knew the perfect disguise for each occasion was to return to Maryland. The most remarkable thing about Harriet's rescue missions is that she never lost a passenger. She was so good at her rescues that people called her "Moses," after the Biblical character who saved the people of Israel from the Egyptian elites who enslaved them.

In 1850, the Fugitive Slave Act was enacted, causing all escaped enslaved people in the North to panic. Harriet's work would become harder and more dangerous. Yet, it didn't stop her. She continued doing good work and offered her services as far as Canada, which was far enough to keep the enslaved people from being recaptured by the U.S. law enforcers' tyranny.

When the American Civil War erupted, Harriet rolled up her sleeves and got to work, serving as a cook, a nurse, and a Union Army spy. With what she knew about traveling with secret routes, she took charge of an armed mission in South Carolina. It was so successful that she set over 700 enslaved people free.

The war ended, and Harriet made her home in Auburn, New York, settling down to care for her parents, who were quite old. She participated in the women's suffrage movement, believing women deserved the right to vote as much as men did. She continued to fight for the freedom and rights of Black American people, contributing to society until she died in 1913. You have to admit Harriet Tubman was a brave, resilient woman.

Famous Quotes

1. *Slavery is the next thing to hell.*
2. *I grew up like a neglected weed, ignorant of liberty, having no experience of it. Then, I was not happy or contented.*
3. *There are two things I've got a right to, and these are Death or Liberty. One or the other, I mean to have.*
4. *I was the conductor of the Underground Railroad for eight years, and I can say what most conductors can't say: I never ran my train off the track, and I never lost a passenger.*
5. *I can't die but once.*

Chapter 3: Unstoppable Minds – Stories of the Smartest People

There have been people with minds so brilliant that even decades after their death, they're still talked about. They've changed the world with their accomplishments and improved the quality of life of millions of people, not because they had excellent ideas but because they were unafraid to explore them further and share their discoveries with the world.

You, too, could be brimming with brilliance. Still, you'll only know if you explore your ideas, share them, and continue following your hunches even when others disagree. Allow these stories to inspire you to share your wonderful ideas with the world.

Albert Einstein

Albert Einstein was born in 1879 in Ulm, Baden-Württemberg, Germany, to Hermann Einstein and Pauline Koch. His dad was an engineer who also worked as a salesperson, while his mother was a housewife caring for the family. Two years after his birth, his sister was born. She was named Maria, but she preferred to go by Maja.

Albert Einstein.

https://commons.wikimedia.org/wiki/File:Albert_Einstein_1921_by_F_Schmutzer.jpg

As brilliant as Einstein is known, he had trouble growing up. He didn't start talking until much later than other children his age. Some sources claim he never spoke a word until he was three. But because he never uttered a word does not mean he wasn't extremely fascinated by the world around him. When he was only five, he found a compass, and all he could think about was how and why the needle moved. This compass was a trigger that encouraged Einstein to study nature and its invisible forces.

Einstein became deeply interested in geometry when he was twelve, as he found a book on the subject that he would later call his "sacred little geometry book." He did terribly in traditional schools for someone with a mind so fascinated by science. He dropped out when he was fifteen because he was doing so poorly. Fortunately, it did not dampen his desire to learn everything about mathematics and physics. He found a way to continue his education.

Einstein set his sights on the Swiss Federal Institute of Technology in Zurich, Switzerland. He wanted to study there, but when he applied, he was denied entry because he failed the examination. He could have called it quits, but he didn't. Instead, he took a year to study at a preparatory school before trying once more to get into the university. This time, he succeeded and gained admission. In 1900, he graduated from the institute and began to teach physics and mathematics.

Einstein found work at the Swiss Patent Office in Bern, where he experienced his "miracle year." (when the most amazing things happen in your life). He had put in a lot of work and published four papers in the German academic journal the Annalen der Physik.

Einstein's publications were remarkable. These ideas he published and shared with the world would later be the foundation for modern physics. The world knows more about space, time, energy, and mass thanks to Einstein. Also, while he didn't like quantum physics, he was a great contributor to that field.

Einstein's first paper described the photoelectric effect, which is about how light and matter interact. This paper was so brilliant it earned him the Nobel Prize in Physics in 1921. His second paper was about Brownian motion, where he gave evidence that atoms are real. In his third paper, he discussed the theory of special relativity, and his final paper was about the equation E = MC2.

Even though Einstein contributed greatly to science, he still struggled in his life. For instance, he kept dealing with academic failures. His equation was flawed because it appeared to work only for particles at rest rather than particles in motion. He spent years figuring out the problem but never did. Max Von Laue solved it six years later.

During the Nazi era, Einstein had to deal with opposition from his political enemies because he was Jewish. The Nazis violated his home and burned his books. One of the most famous Nazi organizations dared to publish a magazine with Einstein's face splashed on the cover and a caption that read "Not Yet Hanged." They put a bounty on his head, which meant Germany was no longer safe for him. He had to flee. So, he did.

Despite everything Einstein faced, he continued with his scientific studies because he was such a curious person. He didn't allow his struggles to faze him. Albert Einstein passed away in 1955 in Princeton, New Jersey. He may be gone, but he lives on in the hearts and minds of many.

Famous Quotes

1. *The true sign of intelligence is not knowledge but imagination.*
2. *There are only two ways to live your life. One is as though nothing is a miracle. The other is as though everything is a miracle.*
3. *I have no special talents. I am only passionately curious.*
4. *Once we accept our limits, we go beyond them.*
5. *A ship is always safe at the shore, but that is not what it is built for.*

Ada Lovelace

Ada Lovelace was born Augusta Ada Byron in 1815 in London, England. She was the daughter of Lord Byron, the famous poet, and Anna Isabella Milbanke, the reformer. Barely a month after her birth, her parents decided it was best to go their separate ways. Lord Byron departed from England forever. Ada never got to know her father personally.

Ada Lovelace.

Antoine Claudet, CC BY-SA 4.0 <https://creativecommons.org/licenses/by-sa/4.0>, via Wikimedia Commons https://commons.wikimedia.org/wiki/File:Ada_Byron_daguerreotype_by_Antoine_Claudet_1843_or_1850_-_cropped.png

Lord Byron's temper was famous. Ada's mother was always worried her daughter might inherit it. So, when Ada showed that she was more interested in logic and mathematics than stirring trouble, her mother breathed a sigh of relief and actively encouraged her to pursue these interests.

Ada's mother felt that the further she could push Ada from the arts, the less likely her daughter would become like her father. Yet this was not enough to keep Ada from being curious about her father, and her interest in him was so great she later named her sons Byron and Gordon.

Ada received private education from tutors and eventually educated herself. She developed an excellent friendship with the British mathematician Charles Babbage, known as the father of computers. Ada and Babbage became fast friends when they met in 1833. At the time, Babbage was known for hosting soirees at night, so Ada and her mother attended one with a mutual friend, Mary Somerville.

As a fellow mathematician, Ada was interested in what Babbage was doing with his Analytical Engine. This engine was a computer, except it was purely mechanical, meaning it could only work with punch cards and other moving parts rather than with software like modern computers.

Unfortunately for Babbage, he didn't have enough funding, so he could not execute his complex designs. He never built a computer that was functional enough for everyday life.

An Italian engineer and mathematician, Luigi Federico Menabrea, wrote an article about Babbage's analytical machine. Curious, Ada translated the article between 1842 and 1843. While translating, she inserted her own notes, leading to a translation thrice as long as the actual article. In her notes, she discussed how it was possible to program the analytical machine to work with Bernoulli numbers, a complex sequence of numbers. Whether Ada realized it or not, she had just written the world's first computer algorithm.

Ada was the first to think of applying the analytical machine to other purposes besides pure calculation. She suggested the machine could work with other things besides numbers, like symbols.

Ada's theories about what the analytical machine could do helped others in her field recognize its potential. She knew if the machine was programmed to follow specific rules, it could run mathematical calculations, create music, and more. And just like that, Ada had theoretically stepped up the machine's abilities from simple calculation to complex computation.

Unfortunately, the world was not ready to accept Ada's deep, amazing contributions to computer science until at least a hundred years after she passed away. She died in 1852. Part of the lack of recognition of her work was that she was in a field where women were not recognized for their brilliance or what they could offer. Now she is celebrated every year on Ada Lovelace Day, held on the second Tuesday of October.

Famous Quotes

1. *I am in a charming state of confusion.*
2. *What is imagination? It is a God-like, noble faculty. It renders earth tolerable. It teaches us to live in the tone of the eternal.*
3. *If you can't give me poetry, can't you give me "poetical science?"*
4. *I don't wish to be without my brains, though they doubtless interfere with blind faith, which would be very comfortable.*
5. *Imagination is the discovering faculty, preeminently. It is that which permeates into the unseen worlds around us, the worlds of science.*

Stephen Hawking

Stephen Hawking was born in Oxford, England, on January 8, 1942. He was the child of Frank and Isabel Hawking. His father worked in medical research, and his mother was one of the first female students to graduate from Oxford. Frank was also an Oxford alumnus.

Stephen Hawking.

https://commons.wikimedia.org/wiki/File:Stephen_Hawking.StarChild.jpg

Hawking's interest in science began at a very young age. He was curious about how things worked and couldn't keep his eyes off the sky. Despite his interest in science, he was nowhere near the top of his class. Still, he maintained his curiosity spirit and always loved thinking outside the box. This was obvious to anyone who knew him. He studied physics at the University College, Oxford, then a PhD at Trinity Hall in Cambridge. It looked like Stephen was ready for greatness.

Unfortunately, in 1963, Stephen was diagnosed with amyotrophic lateral sclerosis (ALS). Doctors were pretty clear about his life expectancy. They didn't see him living beyond the next two years. So, he decided to make those years count by keeping up his research work.

The physics of black holes and the field of general relativity were mainly what Stephen Hawkins studied. His studies led him to discover what he called "Hawking radiation," which happens when black holes leak energy and then fade into nothingness. This was a big deal because, at the time, everyone assumed it was impossible for anything to come out of a black hole.

This brilliant person contributed to the field of quantum physics by sharing his thoughts on the theory of cosmic inflation. According to this theory, after the Big Bang, the universe initially kept expanding rapidly, then slowed down. Stephen also developed the No Boundary theory, which says there's no end or beginning to the universe.

While Stephen continued his work, he suffered greatly from his physical condition. Still, it did not stop him from sharing his ideas on the most advanced and complicated scientific concepts, making it easier for people not in the field to understand.

Hawking published A Brief History of Time in 1988, which became an international bestseller. In the book, he talks about what the universe is made of, where it came from, how it's developed over time, and where it's headed. He shared his thoughts in a way that everyone could appreciate, even if they didn't understand a thing about science.

Stephen Hawking has been recognized by many scientific institutions and organizations with awards. He received the Presidential Medal of Freedom, the highest civilian award offered in the United States of America. He became a Fellow of the Royal Society and was part of the United States National Academy of Sciences. He passed away in 2018, but his life's work lives on in theoretical physics.

Stephen exemplifies what it means to take what you have and make the most out of it. He could have given up on learning and growing when the doctors told him he only had two more years to live, but he decided he was going to make those years count. He should have been gone by 23 but stuck around until 55. It's almost like the secret to the extra 35 years - and you know he made every day count.

Famous Quotes

1. *Life would be tragic if it weren't funny.*
2. *One, remember to look up at the stars and not down at your feet. Two, never give up work. Work gives you meaning and purpose, and life is empty without it. Three, if you are lucky enough to find love, remember it is there, and don't throw it away.*
3. *Without imperfection, you or I would not exist.*
4. *However difficult life may seem, there is always something you can do and succeed at. It matters that you don't just give up.*
5. *My expectations were reduced to zero when I was 21. Everything since then has been a bonus.*

Chapter 4: Young Innovators Just Like You

You don't have to wait until you're old to start on whatever innovative ideas you have. In this chapter, you'll learn about three young individuals who did the most remarkable things before they hit 18.

Once, people believed children couldn't make a difference in the world or contribute much to society until they became adults. These legends will show you all the reasons this thinking is not true. You'll know you don't have to wait until some random age that's "adult enough" to start on the incredible ideas you've kept hidden by the end of this chapter. You can get started right now, as you are.

Boyan Slat

Born in Delft, Netherlands, in 1994, Boyan Slat was always interested in engineering. He constantly came up with new inventions. Boyan's life took an interesting turn at 16 when he went on vacation to Greece. He decided it would be fun to go scuba diving but wasn't prepared for what he'd find.

Boyan Slat.

DWDD, CC BY 3.0 <https://creativecommons.org/licenses/by/3.0>, via Wikimedia Commons. https://commons.wikimedia.org/wiki/File:Boyan_Slat_(2018).jpg

To Boyan's dismay, the sea had more plastic than fish. You can imagine how disappointing it must have been to expect to see various sea creatures only to find they've been replaced by trash. One question bothered Boyan: Why didn't people clean the sea?

Boyan was no ordinary person. Unlike most people, he didn't ask his questions, only to forget about them. He pondered it, dreaming up possible solutions. His question remained front and center in his mind for long enough to make him take action. He did a high school project on why the ocean is so polluted with plastic. But that wasn't enough for Boyan. He needed to know what could be done with technology to make the ocean as clean and safe for marine life as it once was.

In 2012, Boyan attended a TedX Conference in Delft, where he shared his ideas with the world. What did he come up with? He thought of a passive plastic catchment system to clean the ocean - just like a large net catches leaves in a flowing stream.

Boyan's system is a huge arm stretching out on the water's surface, with a skirt hanging from it. The plastic waste gets caught in the skirt when the waves push the barrier around. The wonderful thing about Boyan's contraption is that it doesn't need electricity to operate. It works fine on its own, letting the endless ocean waves do the work. The plastic waste is later collected and recycled. This way, the ocean stays clean. And just like that, Boyan helped solve a problem affecting every nation in the world.

Boyan didn't abandon his idea. He kept looking for ways to make it better. So, he dropped out of Delft University of Technology to improve his fantastic contraption. At the time, he only had 300 Euros to his name, but Boyan knew he could make his dream happen.

Soon, he founded The Ocean Cleanup, a nonprofit organization for developing newer, better ways to remove plastic from every ocean. His organization raised $2.2 million thanks to a crowdfunding campaign.

With Boyan leading, The Ocean Cleanup got 18,000 people from 160 countries to contribute to cleaning the oceans. Boyan's nonprofit created a floater 600 meters long, with a skirt 3 meters deep to hold plastic waste. Since the system doesn't move as fast as the water, it's easy for the water to flow through it while leaving the plastic trapped in the skirt. Was this such an easy thing to accomplish? It wasn't.

Boyan's The Ocean Cleanup first devised two systems: System 001 and System 001/B. Sadly, they didn't work as well as he and his team had hoped because so many things kept breaking down. Yet, Boyan didn't let this discourage him or his team. Instead, they focused on what went wrong so they could learn from their mistakes and correct them as needed. They finally solved System 001/B's issues in 2019, which worked perfectly well this time.

Even now, Boyan and his nonprofit organization, The Ocean Cleanup, are doing great work eliminating the huge mess in the ocean known as the Great Pacific Garbage Patch. They've even found ways to keep plastic from getting into the ocean. By 2040, Boyan and his team intend to remove at least 90 percent of the floating plastic polluting the ocean. Boyan Slat's story shows you're never too young to make a difference, and when you learn from your mistakes, you'll find the solutions to your problems.

Famous Quotes

1. *For society to progress, we should not only move forward but also clean up after ourselves.*

2. *There's no better feeling than having an idea and seeing it become reality, emerging in the physical world.*
3. *I really hate looking back. I think it's useless. The only way is forward.*
4. *Everyone once said to me, "Oh, there's nothing you can do about plastic once it gets into the oceans," and I wondered whether that was true.*
5. *I don't understand why obsessive has a negative connotation. I'm obsessive, and I like it. I get an idea, and I stick to it.*

Gitanjali Rao

Gitanjali Rao is another phenomenal person who left her mark on the world at a young age. She was born in Columbus, Ohio, in 2005 to Bharathi and Ram Rao. She moved from Ohio to Lone Tree, Colorado, and attended STEM School Highlands Ranch. Even as a young child, her love and passion for science were profound. It started when she was 4 years old, and her uncle gifted her a science kit.

Gitanjali Rao.

When Gitanjali was ten years old, she discovered the Flint water crisis, thanks to the news. From then on, the only thing she could think about was how she could measure how much lead was in the water so people would know how polluted it was and stay safe. She thought long and worked hard, and when she was 12, she devised Tethys, a portable device for testing lead in water.

She made Tethys with carbon nanotubes, which send lead-level information to a processor via Bluetooth. How did she figure out she could use carbon nanotubes to create her device? She studied information from the Massachusetts Institute of Technology as part of her research. Once she succeeded at her goal, she worked with scientists, doctors, and others in the medical profession to see how Tethys could help them.

In 2017, Gitanjali was the Discovery Education 3M Young Scientist Challenge winner and went home with a whopping $25,000 for inventing Tethys. She presented the device at the 2018 MAKERS Conference and received another $25,000. In January 2019, she worked with the Denver water facility to create an improved version of her device over the next two years.

Gitanjali developed other inventions besides Tethys. For instance, she invented Epione in 2019, a tool that helps medical professionals diagnose addiction to prescription opioids as early as possible. Unstoppable, Gitanjali also devised Kindly, an app that uses artificial intelligence to catch cyberbullies and stop them before they cause too much damage. She partnered with UNICEF to make this app available to the world.

The wonderful thing about Gitanjali's story is how she never let her age make her believe she couldn't do great things for humanity. For this, she received recognition as America's Top Young Scientist. She got an EPA Presidential award for Tethys. Even Time Magazine featured her in 2020 as the first ever Kid of the Year because of how she used technology to solve worldly problems. How awesome is that?

Famous Quotes

1. *If I can do it, you can do it, and anyone can do it.*
2. *My goal has really shifted, not only from creating my own devices to solve the world's problems but inspiring others to do the same as well.*
3. *I believe that each one of us can take small steps to address the problems with whatever talents we have.*
4. *I really hope the work that all of these kids are doing identifies innovation as a necessity and not something that's a choice anymore. I hope I can be a small part of that.*

5. *Innovation doesn't have a deadline. So, when I start going, I can keep going, and there's no one stopping me.*

Jack Andraka

Jack Thomas Andraka was born in Crownsville, Maryland, in 1997. Like Gitanjali, he developed an interest in science from a young age. How did his journey to greatness begin? In the spring of 2011, tragedy struck when he lost his close family friend who had been battling pancreatic cancer. This lit a fire in Jack's heart to find better ways to detect the presence of this disease than what was available. He discovered how at 15.

Jack Andraka.

XPRIZE Foundation, CC BY 2.0 <https://creativecommons.org/licenses/by/2.0>, via Wikimedia Commons. https://commons.wikimedia.org/wiki/File:Jack_Andraka_2013.jpg

Jack's device helps detect cancer when it's still early enough for something to be done to stop it. The device has a sensor like those used in diabetic test strips. This sensor has filter paper with carbon nanotubes and antibodies that fight against mesothelin in humans. The device analyzes the amounts of mesothelin in the body to deduce if cancer is present. This was a method unlike anything ever created.

Jack had somehow developed a way to detect cancer 168 times faster than the current methods. Moreover, his method was only 1/26667 times the cost of testing and had 4000 times the sensitivity of the ELISA cancer detection method, which was in use at the time.

Was it easy for Jack to come up with his cancer testing method? Not at all. The scientific community didn't take him seriously. The scientist who discovered mesothelin, Ira Pastan, claimed there was nothing sensible or logical about Jack's idea. Ira added that he didn't know anyone in the scientific community who would believe anything Jack had to share.

Another critic of Jack's was George M. Church, an American geneticist and professor at Harvard University. George was worried about the claims of Jack's method, as he didn't believe it could work that fast, was that sensitive to mesothelin, and so cheap.

But Jack didn't let the naysayers get him down. He could have said his critics were right since they were older and more experienced. He could have quit, But Jack wasn't the type to give up. Instead, he kept going. Anirban Maitra, a Johns Hopkins School of Medicine professor, supervised him.

Jack patented his device and reached out to companies to create a version everyone could buy over the counter at the pharmacist's without going to the hospital.

Jack Andraka's work was so phenomenal he was given the Gordon E. Moore Award at the Intel International Science and Engineering Fair. Never let anyone dampen your curiosity, whether they think you can make your dreams come true or not. Keep going, not to prove them wrong, but to prove yourself right.

Famous Quotes

1. *Embrace the "what if?"*
2. *It doesn't matter what your age, gender, or race is. It's your ideas that count.*
3. *I learned that with the Internet, anything is possible.*
4. *You don't have to be a professor with multiple degrees to have your idea work.*
5. *Anticipate failure and then briskly push it aside to keep moving forward. You learn from your failures.*

Chapter 5: Champions of Kindness

It's wonderful to be kind. A little kindness can go a long way toward changing the world and making it a lovely place for everyone. Kindness is powerful. Whether being kind to someone or someone else has done something that warms your heart, there's something about this way of life that makes life more fulfilling. When you tap into the kindness within you like the people in this chapter did, you'll be amazed and delighted by how your kind choices improve the lives of the people around you and yours, too. That's the thing about choosing kindness every time - and the best part? It doesn't cost a thing.

Mother Teresa

Anjezë Gonxhe Bojaxhiu was born in 1910 in North Macedonia, a little town known as Skopje. What set this little girl apart from others was her big, warm heart. She was such a caring person who expressed her love for others through kind, compassionate acts.

Mother Teresa.

Kingkongphoto & www.celebrity-photos.com from Laurel, Maryland, USA, CC BY-SA 2.0 <https://creativecommons.org/licenses/by-sa/2.0>, via Wikimedia Commons. https://commons.wikimedia.org/wiki/File:Mother_Teresa_1.jpg

At 18, something was tugging Anjezë toward the church. She wanted nothing more than to serve God, so she made the tough decision to leave her family and the home she knew and loved behind. She joined the Sisters of Loreto in Ireland and adopted the name she is most commonly known by. She became Sister Mary Teresa, named after Saint Thérèse of Lisieux.

Sister Mary Teresa's service took her as far as Kolkata in India, a land of many people - and double the suffering. She wanted to help them and decided to teach at Saint Mary's School. As she worked there, she couldn't help but notice the many people battling sickness and poverty right outside the walls of the school where she taught. She felt she had to do something more.

In 1948, Sister Teresa realized there was only one way she could do more. She had to leave the convent. She rolled up her sleeves and helped the poor who couldn't afford to care for themselves. Leaving the convent meant she had to stop wearing her nun's habit. She had a different uniform now. It was a white sari with a blue border, an outfit that would later remind the world of who she was and what she accomplished. She became known as Mother Teresa.

Two years after leaving the convent, she set up the Missionaries of Charity with only 12 members. Now, the organization has members in over 130 countries, helping the sick and dying, doing what they can for schools, clinics, and orphanages that need support.

Mother Teresa and her fellow sisters never rested too long as they nurtured those who needed their help. They gave love to those who felt lost and alone, cared for people too sick to do anything about their health, and fed those starving. Somehow, they accomplished all of this without having many resources. How did they pull this off? They shared the little they had. Their kindness inspired those who witnessed it to do what they could to help.

Helping the helpless isn't easy work. So, the world celebrates Mother Teresa and appreciates her generosity and kindness. In 1979, she was awarded a Nobel Peace Prize. She received many other awards but didn't care for them or the recognition. All the good Mother wanted was to serve God by helping others around her.

Whenever you feel there's no point in helping others because you think what you have to offer isn't much, remember what Mother Teresa realized: A little goes a long way. Don't be afraid to share what you can. Your kindness will give someone a brighter day.

Famous Quotes

1. *Small things done with great love will change the world.*
2. *If you are kind, people may accuse you of selfish, ulterior motives. Be kind anyway.*
3. *The good you do today will often be forgotten by tomorrow. Do good anyway.*
4. *I can do things you cannot. You can do things I cannot. Together, we can do great things.*
5. *Yesterday is gone. Tomorrow has not yet come. We have only today. Let us begin.*

Fred Rogers

Fred was born in Latrobe, Pennsylvania, in 1928. His full name was Fred McFeely Rogers. His childhood was riddled with problems because he was always sick, which meant he spent most days resting in bed. Yet, he didn't let his constant sickness make him sad or blue. Instead, he had fun imagining magical worlds with interesting characters.

Fred Rogers.

https://commons.wikimedia.org/wiki/File:Fred_Rogers_and_Tatiana_Vedeneyeva_on_Set_of_Mister_Rogers%27_Neighborhood_(cropped).jpg

When Fred was older and went to college, he studied music since he enjoyed writing songs and playing the piano. Fred's life would turn the first time he saw a television. What he saw on the screen didn't impress him - people were throwing pies at one another. Others may have thought this was funny, but Fred was different. He wanted to use the television to help children discover the beautiful things about the world and learn more about themselves.

When Fred Rogers graduated from college, he joined NBC in New York City to start his TV career. But he realized he didn't enjoy commercial TV. So, he moved back home and created Pittsburgh's WQED, a TV station run and supported by the community. It was the first of its kind in America.

The first time Fred Rogers was on camera was on a program called Misterogers, an earlier version of Mister Rogers' Neighborhood. Eventually, Fred Rainsberry of the Canadian Broadcasting System noticed Fred and asked him to host his show in Canada.

When Fred returned to the US, he created the Mister Rogers' Neighborhood show on the Eastern Educational Television Network. His first show aired on February 19, 1968. His show was a safe space for every child. He kicked off each episode by wearing a simple sweater and sneakers and singing, "Won't You Be My Neighbor?" One thing kids and adults loved about his show was how relaxing it was. Other shows were loud and had fancy, flashy animation, but that wasn't what Mr. Rogers was about.

On Fred's show, his voice was always soft and soothing to everyone watching. The way he treated children showed that he respected them. He was always kind and considerate, the picture of a good neighbor.

On his show, Fred helped children understand their feelings, whether they were scared, angry, hurt, or sad. He helped children learn how to handle their emotions healthily. He helped children understand how to handle difficult problems like disabilities, divorce, and death. It was a wholesome show.

Sometimes, Mr. Rogers would take the kids on virtual field trips so they'd learn certain jobs, how things are made, different art and music genres, and rich cultures all over the world. He never missed a chance to let the children know they were perfect the way they were and didn't have to be someone other than themselves.

Sadly, Fred Rogers died on February 27, 2003, yet his kindness still touches people. Everyone, young or old, still loves his shows. There's no way you grew up watching Mr. Rogers and don't smile or feel good when remembering your favorite episodes. He was gentle and kind as he taught people about the world and themselves, as he'd always wanted to do.

Famous Quotes

1. *Often when you think you're at the end of something, you're at the beginning of something else.*
2. *You make each day a special day. You know how, by just being you.*
3. *There are three ways to ultimate success. The first way is to be kind. The second way is to be kind. The third way is to be kind.*
4. *We live in a world in which we need to share responsibility.*
5. *If you could only sense how important you are to the lives of those you meet,*
6. *how important you can be to the people you may never even dream of.*

Irena Sendler

Born in Warsaw, Poland, in 1910, Irena Stanislawa Sendler was a shining example of being kind, even when it meant getting into trouble. She was a light that shined during the darkest times when many lives were lost because some people refused to see others as equal. She was a brave woman who never let anything get in her way as she fought for good and equality, even when many wanted her silenced.

Irena Sendler.

Mariusz Kubik, zoom by User:ABX, CC BY 3.0 <https://creativecommons.org/licenses/by/3.0>, *via Wikimedia Commons* https://commons.wikimedia.org/wiki/File:Irena_Sendlerowa_2005-02-13_zoom.jpg

Irena's dad, Stanisław Henryk Krzyżanowski, was a physician, so she watched him help many people. She admired him and learned how important it was to assist those who couldn't care for themselves or deal with their problems. Watching her father work lit a fire in her heart to give back to people in any way she could.

In the 30s, Irena was a social worker and an activist working with the Free Polish University. She worked for the Department of Social Welfare and Public Health of the City of Warsaw between 1935 and 1948. Among the activists in Żegota - the Polish Council to Aid Jews created in 1942 - Irena was not only present but also the head of the organization. In 1943, she took over as the leader of the Children's Section, too.

Irena was well known, so she had many people in various institutions and orphanages to help her keep the precious children hidden from the Nazis. This woman worked tirelessly with others to help Jewish children escape the Warsaw Ghetto. She provided whatever was needed to ensure the children would find safety. If they needed identity papers, she would secure them. If they needed a place to rest their heads, she would find Polish families who were aligned with her cause and would willingly open their doors to these children.

When she couldn't find families, Irena looked for care facilities and orphanages to care for the precious children. She also worked hard with the Catholic nun convents to get these children far from the clutches of the Nazis. It was thanks to her heroic efforts that these children were saved from the horrendous effects of the Holocaust.

Unfortunately, Irena was eventually caught by the Gestapo in October 1943. They were cruel to her. While in prison, they tortured her, hoping she would reveal everything about the children she'd saved and where to find them. Despite how much they tortured her, she kept her lips sealed. The Gestapo realized they would never get a word out of her and sentenced her to death. Fortunately, the day Irena was to be executed, she escaped. Thankfully, Żegota had bribed the right Germans to release her.

After the war, Irena continued to be a social activist. She knew there was a lot of work to be done. She knew she'd make the most progress by joining the government. In 1965, Israel recognized Irena Sendler as Righteous Among the Nations. She passed away in 2008, but her legacy is alive and well. Thousands of people owe their lives to her. Let the life of this outstanding woman remind you that kindness matters and that there'll never be a good enough reason to stop being kind to the people around you.

Famous Quotes

1. *People can only be divided into good or bad; their race, religion, and nationality don't matter.*
2. *The term "hero" irritates me greatly.*
3. *Every child saved with my help and the help of all these wonderful secret messengers, who today are no longer living, is the justification of my existence on this earth and not a title to glory.*
4. *You see a man drowning, you must try to save him even if you cannot swim.*
5. *Fear makes you weak; anger makes you strong.*

Chapter 6: Creative Inspirations: Artists and Inventors

Your creativity is a precious, powerful thing. Whatever interests you, whether science, mathematics, finances, or another aspect of life, there's always room to express your strange yet brilliant ideas. Give yourself permission to explore what you can do and to do things in new, better, or different ways you or others haven't thought of before (even if it seems silly or weird).

So many inventions you enjoy today exist because someone dared to think outside the box. In this chapter, you'll read stories of artists and inventors who had exceptional creativity and weren't afraid to push the limits.

Leonardo da Vinci

Leonardo da Vinci was born in 1452 in Anchiano, Tuscany, now Italy. He was a true Renaissance man. What does that mean? Leonardo was great at many things. He loved to give his mind a workout by learning new ideas and subjects he'd never known before. Leonardo was an engineer, inventor, architect, and painter. If you could ask him right now, he'd tell you he considered himself a lifelong student.

Leonardo da Vinci.

https://commons.wikimedia.org/wiki/File:Possible_Self-Portrait_of_Leonardo_da_Vinci.jpg

You'd be correct if you think that Leonardo must have been a genius. It's not that he understood various unrelated topics, but he was quite good in each field. It's hard to find someone who doesn't know about his famous paintings like the Last Supper and the Mona Lisa, two paintings representing the unbeatable quality of his work in everything he did.

Leonardo's parents never married. His father worked as a notary and an attorney, and his mother was a peasant. Leonardo grew up in his father's family estate in Vinci. He knew how to read, write, and solve mathematics but didn't get a formal education.

Fortunately, Leonardo's father realized he was extremely talented in art, so he let Leonardo become an apprentice to the renowned sculptor and painter Andrea del Verrocchio of Florence when he was 15. For the next 10 years, he worked on his sculpting and painting style, getting better each year. He also worked on mechanical arts.

In 1472, Leonardo turned 20. He was offered Painters' Guild of Florence membership but declined. He chose to remain with his master, Verrocchio, until he was ready to become an independent master six years later.

In 1482, he started on his first commissioned work, the Adoration of the Magi. This work was for the Monastery of San Donato a Scopeto in Florence. Unfortunately, he never finished this piece because he had to travel to Milan shortly after starting to work for the Sforza clan, who ruled Milan. There, he designed the court festivals and served as an architect, painter, engineer, and, more often than not, a sculptor.

It's amazing how much Leonardo was able to get done, considering it's believed he had attention deficit hyperactivity disorder or ADHD. ADHD is a disorder that makes it hard to focus or pay attention. Sometimes, it causes you to be so hyperactive you can't settle down to work. Other times, it can make you act impulsively, even if it means you will regret your choices later.

As if that wasn't enough, Leonardo was also dyslexic. When you have dyslexia, it's hard to read, write, and spell correctly. But he didn't let these challenges keep him from channeling his creativity into his art.

Leonardo lived during a time when it wasn't common to be self-taught. If you didn't go to school, you'd be considered weird. He never let this problem get in his way. Being self-taught meant he could learn things at his own pace and in the best way for him.

This artist struggled with money. Leonardo's livelihood depended on wealthy people taking an interest in his work. He wasn't the only artist, so he constantly competed with others. He lived during much political unrest. Various city-states kept shifting their alliances, being friends one day and enemies the next, making it hard for him to find stable work.

As any artist will tell you, criticism and rejection are part of the game. Whether you're a writer, painter, dancer, designer, or anything else, your work will get criticized. Some people will love it, others won't because art is purely subjective - what looks beautiful to one person looks hideous to another.

The great Leonardo was also rejected and criticized. Little did his critics know how great and legendary his work would become years later. His work was criticized heavily because he used techniques and ideas beyond his time. He saw the future before others did. He could have stopped going against the grain and returned to creating art like everyone else. Still, he didn't let other people's opinions keep him from continuing on his path.

Besides the Last Supper and the Mona Lisa, Leonardo is known for the Vitruvian Man, Lady with an Ermine, and The Annunciation. If you look at the notebooks he kept, you'd realize this was a man who loved to ask scientific questions. The things he thought about were eons ahead of his time.

Leo thought about creating a parachute, even though there was no use for it back then. He also imagined an armored fighting truck and a helicopter. He had ideas about creating cars and using concentrated solar and steam power.

Leonardo didn't care too much about money, but he was generous toward his friends and those who helped him. He died at age 67 in 1519, spending the last of his years in Amboise, France, where King Francis I patronized him. When he passed away, he'd thought that he hadn't left a mark on the world, but he had no idea how wrong he was. Centuries later, Leonardo's work and brilliant mind are still celebrated.

Famous Quotes

1. *Art is never finished, only abandoned.*
2. *Learning never exhausts the mind.*
3. *Nothing strengthens authority so much as silence.*
4. *Time stays long enough for anyone who will use it.*
5. *Why does the eye see a thing more clearly in dreams than the imagination when awake?*

Frida Kahlo

Frida Kahlo was born in 1907 in Coyoacan, Mexico. Her father was German with Hungarian roots, while her mother was Mexican with Native American and Spanish roots. Frida was closer to her dad than her mother and helped him with his photography. She learned how to spot details working with him in the studio.

Frida Kahlo.

https://commons.wikimedia.org/wiki/File:Frida_Kahlo,_by_Guillermo_Kahlo_(cropped).jpg

She took a few classes in drawing but wasn't as interested as she was in science. She got into the National Preparatory School in Mexico City because of her interest in science and hoped to study medicine afterward. Frida was one of 35 female students in a school of 2000 students. She wasn't afraid to speak her mind, and people knew her for her bravery.

A terrible incident would change Frida's plans for medicine. In 1925, she had an accident so bad she needed over 30 operations at different stages in her life. As she recovered from the accident, she was drawn to art again, like when she was a child, so she decided to become an artist instead.

Kahlo was interested in the political scene, so in 1927, she became part of the Mexican Communist Party. There, she met another artist, Diego Rivera. They fell in love, married in 1929, and toured Mexico and the United States throughout the late 20s and early 30s, enjoying their life together.

If you study Frida's art, you'll notice she had a way of painting things that could only have come from a dream. Her work was magical. She painted many portraits of herself, various symbols representing what it means to be a woman in a man's world, surviving losing important things and people and dealing with traumatic, difficult experiences.

She found a way to combine fantasy and real life in her work. This is why her art is called magical realism or surrealism. Living in Mexico, her work carried a lot of colors that popped, and the symbols made you stop, stare, and think.

Frida didn't have an easy life. She struggled with polio as a child, and then the bus accident caused her so many health problems. Still, she didn't let any of it stop her from expressing her true self to the world through her painting. She discovered she could take all her pain and sadness and put it into her work, making her feel better and giving others something they could relate to.

When Frida Kahlo passed away in 1954, her death shook the art world. Her work is still influential, inspiring many artists. Her life is studied by sociologists and psychologists even today. Dr. Fernando Antelo, a forensic pathology fellow, studied Frida's art and realized she'd brilliantly added a bit of science to her artwork, like fetuses in the womb or the pain experienced from health problems.

Famous Quotes

1. *Nothing is absolute. Everything changes, everything moves, everything evolves, everything flies and goes away.*
2. *There is nothing more precious than laughter. It is strength to laugh and lose oneself, to be light.*
3. *Everything can have beauty, even the worst horror.*
4. *Fall in love with yourself, with life, and then with whoever you want.*
5. *What would I do without the absurd and the ephemeral?*

Tim Berners-Lee

Don't you just love that the Internet exists? Imagine a world without it. Sure, humans didn't need the Internet to survive once upon a time, but it's a different story today. In many ways, the world is better thanks to the World Wide Web. So, who do you thank for the marvelous miracle of the Internet? It's Tim Berners-Lee, born in 1955 in London, England. His mother and father were Mary Lee Woods and Conway Berners-Lee. They were computer scientists and mathematicians from Birmingham and part of the group that created the first-ever commercial computer, the Ferranti Mark I.

Tim Berners Lee.

Tim attended Sheen Mount Primary School and then the Emanuel School in London, where he remained from 1969 to 1973. Afterward, he studied at the University of Oxford's "The Queen's College" in 1973. Three years later, he graduated first-class, proving he was a brilliant mind.

Tim had always dreamed about creating a space where people all over the world could share information freely. He developed his World Wide Web idea while at the Conseil Européen pour la Recherche Nucléaire (CERN). He wanted a way to make it easy for scientists worldwide to share what they knew with each other.

Tim dreamed of his system being automatic and figured he could combine links you click on, internet connections, and computer technology to make a system that helped people share their knowledge.

Tim drafted his first proposal to create the World Wide Web in 1989, but nothing happened. He wrote another one in 1990, and this time, everything worked out. He had set up the first server and browser at CERN, showing other scientists the potential of his ideas.

Tim Berners-Lee did all his coding for the server using a NeXT computer created by Steve Jobs. It would have been a disaster if the computer had been switched off while he worked. What did he do to keep this from happening? He stuck a label on the computer with bold red writing that read, "This machine is a server. DO NOT POWER IT DOWN!!" Thankfully, no one did.

Tim worked long and hard on numerous ways to allow different computers to interact with each other and give the researchers the power to control machines that weren't physically in the room. His ideas changed the world forever. Queen Elizabeth II awarded him a knighthood, a very honorable title to receive from the Queen of England. He received the Millennium Technology Prize from the Finnish Technology Award Foundation. The prize was a whopping €1 million.

Life wasn't always easy for Tim. If there's one thing he's always struggled with, it's his tendency to overthink. He always needs to understand why things are the way they are, so making decisions is hard.

Still, Tim found a way to turn this challenge to his advantage. Rather than work against his weakness, he accepted it and made it work for him, and his efforts were worth it.

His work changed how people connect, making it much easier to share information. Many years ago, you'd have to wait to receive letters by "snail mail," meaning you could wait days or even weeks until you received a note from a loved one. Now, everyone's only a DM or an internet call away, making the world a more connected space. Thanks to Tim Berners-Lee and his World Wide Web, you can learn how to build a rocket or spend all day having a blast on TikTok.

Famous Quotes

1. *The Web, as I envisaged it, we have not seen it yet. The future is still so much bigger than the past.*
2. *We need diversity of thought in the world to face new challenges.*
3. *When something is such a creative medium as the web, the limits to it are our imagination.*
4. *We can't blame the technology when we make mistakes.*
5. *Anyone who has lost track of time when using a computer knows the propensity to dream, the urge to make dreams come true, and the tendency to miss lunch.*

Chapter 7: Nurturing Nature – Heroes of the Earth

Earth is your home. It's also home to everyone else. There's no other place to be but here, so it matters that everyone does their part to care for this planet. Some people only talk about doing something to save the Earth, but others take action.

These people do something to make life on this little blue dot better each day for everyone because of their selfless devotion to fighting against climate change. In this chapter, you'll read about three amazing people who have made their mark in the world because they decided to care for Mother Earth, which humans call home.

David Attenborough

David Attenborough was born in 1926 in London, England. He's an author, natural historian, biologist, and broadcaster. This is what it means to be prolific or good at everything. His family was accomplished in academics. His dad and mom were principals of Leicester's University College at different times.

David Attenborough.

John Cairns, CC BY 4.0 <https://creativecommons.org/licenses/by/4.0>, via Wikimedia Commons.
https://commons.wikimedia.org/wiki/File:Sir_David_Frederick_Attenborough_at_Weston_Library_Opening_20.3.15_(cropped).jpg

David's parents loved learning and reading, and he picked this up. He loved learning about the world and explored it every chance as a child. He collected stones and fossils for fun. David's older brother Richard took a different path, though. He decided to be an actor and movie producer and did well for himself.

As for David, his heart lay with natural history, as it always had since he was a young boy. So, when he was accepted into Clare College, Cambridge, he studied Natural Sciences.

Once he graduated in 1947, he spent two years serving in the Royal Navy. Afterward, David worked with the British Broadcasting Corporation (BBC) to create TV shows educating people about nature. He explored the world, from deep oceans and dense jungles to high mountains and bare deserts. He showed the world the unique creatures he found along the way.

Working with Jack Lester, a reptile curator, David created a TV show, Zoo Quest, in 1954, where he'd show the animals in the zoo and the wild. The BBC appreciated this show because it was a great way to educate children about the natural world.

Eleven years later, David became the controller of BBC-2, the BBC's second TV channel. He produced The Forsyte Saga, Kenneth Clark's

Civilization, and Jacob Bronowski's The Ascent of Man. He also aired Monty Python's Flying Circus, an excellent comedy series.

After spending four years working as the BBC's director of television programming, David decided it was time to move on to other things. So, in 1972, he resigned to focus on his writing and to create TV series as a freelancer. He has an impressive collection of film credits as a presenter, narrator, and writer, especially since he has worked for over 80 years. He's responsible for the Planet Earth franchise, Wildlife on One, Natural World, The Blue Planet, and many other shows. Besides David Attenborough, no one else can boast about winning the BAFTA Awards in 4k, 3D, high-definition, color, and black and white.

David's "Life" series is one of his most famous works. It was a documentary series on mother nature, showing everything there was to discover about animals. He covered everything from whales to insects and made you feel like you weren't just watching him on TV but right there with him, observing the animals in their natural habitat.

If you think David's work was all rainbows and unicorns, think again. It was tough and demanding since he had to visit some of the most remote places, and sometimes, he'd have run-ins with animals that could have made a snack out of him if he weren't careful. Also, the weather wasn't always great. Yet, none of these challenges kept David from exploring the world and showing people why caring for the environment mattered. He saw everything about nature as beautiful - even the dangerous parts.

David had challenges working at the BBC. When he first joined them, they barely had programming about nature, so he had to work hard to convince them it was worth the time and money. As if that weren't enough, David had a boss who told him he couldn't be on TV because he thought his teeth were too big. That's not a very kind thing to say to someone. Yet, David believed in himself, and it paid off.

Today, he continues to speak up for the Earth, calling everyone to do their part. He is concerned about climate change and wants nothing more than to leave the planet in a good state so future generations can enjoy it as you do now.

Through David Attenborough's words, he has stirred many people all over the world to do their part to end activities leading to climate change. His remarkable legacy has been recognized with many awards for his hard work. He received a knighthood in the United Kingdom.

Famous Quotes

1. *It is that range of biodiversity that we must care for - the whole thing, rather than just one or two stars.*
2. *I wish the world was twice as big - and half of it was still unexplored.*
3. *Young people - they care. They know that this is the world that they're going to grow up in, that they're going to spend the rest of their lives in. But I think it's more idealistic than that. They actually believe that humanity, the human species, has no right to destroy and despoil regardless.*
4. *The whole of life is coming to terms with yourself and the natural world. Why are you here? How do you fit in? What's it all about?*
5. *This is a story of our changing planet and what we can do to help it thrive.*

Greta Thunberg

Greta Tintin Eleonora Ernman Thunberg was born in 2003 in Stockholm, Sweden, to an actor and an opera singer. Greta was diagnosed with Asperger syndrome, now recognized as an autism spectrum disorder. With this condition, you become fixed on one interest or idea and nothing else.

Greta Thunberg.

For Greta, nothing was as interesting to her as climate change. It was a topic near and dear to Greta's heart. She was so invested in climate change solutions she stopped going to school regularly at 15. Rather than goof off, she spent her time outside the Swedish parliament, making her voice heard. She carried a sign that read "Skolstrejk för Klimatet," meaning "school strike for climate."

Eventually, Greta would become more regular with her school attendance. Still, she always skipped classes on Friday to resume her strike. She called these days "Fridays for Future." Thankfully, she was able to graduate from school in 2023 despite skipping classes. Greta has always advocated relentlessly for something to be done about climate change. She'd eventually turn Fridays for Future into a movement in 2018.

At what point did Greta become a true activist? She started with her parents, encouraging them to change their lifestyle choices to reduce their home's carbon footprint, and kept going until she became internationally famous. Greta is the influencer other influencers wish they could be. She was so good at persuading people that her influence was called "the Greta Effect."

In 2019, she was acknowledged as the youngest-ever Time Person of the Year. She has received several nominations for the Nobel Peace Prize, won the Right Livelihood Award (the Alternative Nobel Prize), and bagged Amnesty International's Ambassador of Conscience award.

As awesome as all these awards and nominations are, they aren't why Greta got involved in the climate change movement. She's always believed handling the climate change crisis with the same urgency and importance as other issues the world is facing is crucial. She wants to keep future generations safe from the effects of terrible choices that hurt the environment.

Greta has been fighting the good fight, but it hasn't been easy by any means. She has had to stand trial because she attended protests that obstructed important conferences and refused to leave. For instance, the London Trial in February 2024. Why? She and over two dozen protesters blocked the entrance to a conference involving the heavyweights in the oil and gas industry. They were arrested on October 17 because they didn't allow the Energy Intelligence Forum conference attendees to get into the hotel.

During this protest, Greta and her supporters lit colorful flares and played drums loudly to disrupt activities at the hotel. Some protesters rappelled from the hotel's roof - if you can believe it! Eventually, the police had to step in to restore order. But the police weren't successful because even though they kept arresting protesters, new ones arrived on the scene to replace those captured. This kept happening and created a never-ending loop known as a perpetual cycle.

Soon, there were far too many protesters, and the police couldn't keep up because there weren't enough officers to arrest them. The perpetual cycle kept going for five hours. The police were left with no choice but to ask the demonstrators to continue their protest on an adjacent street.

While other protesters complied with the police, Greta didn't. She bravely remained in front of the hotel's entrance. After one last warning from law enforcement officers, she was arrested. This is only one of several trials Greta has faced because of her passion for climate change issues.

This trial lasted two days, and eventually, Greta was charged with breaching a section of the Public Order Act along with four other protesters. The police are legally allowed to put a limit on public assemblies. Since Greta and the other protesters did not comply, they had to stand trial.

Fortunately, the judge ruled that there wasn't enough evidence from the Crown to prove their case against Greta and the protesters. The judge also reprimanded the police because the conditions they put on the protesters were not clear, meaning their arrest was not fair since Greta and her people had done nothing wrong.

Regardless of the loud voices opposing Greta, she continues to be a powerful advocate for fixing climate change. Thanks to her work and her unwillingness to be silenced, she has inspired youth all over the world to do their part in fighting the issues threatening Earth and every human on it. You, too, can be like Greta. Speak up without fear, and you'll be surprised by how far you'll go.

Famous Quotes

1. *Once we start to act, hope is everywhere. So, instead of looking for hope, look for action. Then, and only then, hope will come.*
2. *I see the world in black and white, and I don't like compromising.*

3. *Giving up cannot be an option.*
4. *We should no longer measure our wealth and success in the graph that shows economic growth but in the curve that shows the emissions of greenhouse gases.*
5. *Why should I be studying for a future that soon may not exist?*

Wangari Maathai

Wangari Maathai was born in 1940 in Nyeri, Kenya, in a little village called Ihithe. She was part of the Kikuyu ethnic group and was known for being an environmental activist and scholar. She is the first woman to get a doctorate in Central and East Africa. Back then, it was rare to find girls going to school in Kenya. Thankfully, that has changed.

Wangari Maathai.

Oregon State University, ATTRIBUTION-SHAREALIKE 2.0 GENERIC, CC BY-SA 2.0 <https://creativecommons.org/licenses/by-sa/2.0/> https://www.flickr.com/photos/oregonstateuniversity/6673976497

In 1964, Wangari studied Biology at Mount St. Scholastica College in the United States, now the Benedictine College. Then, she went to the University of Pittsburgh to get her master's in biology in 1966. In 1971, she got a PhD at the University of Nairobi.

After her studies, Wangari dedicated herself to teaching. She was part of the Department of Veterinary Anatomy at the University of Nairobi. Six years after graduation, she was promoted and became the department's chair. But she wasn't only about school, learning, and lecturing. She was a fighter, a warrior who battled to preserve the environment and secure women's rights.

Wangari looked around her lovely childhood home and realized something sinister was happening. When she was a child, her land was full of beautiful, lush green forests that thrived and blessed the people and the animals who made them their home. But she realized those forests were disappearing, and the animals and people who had always depended on them suffered. So Wangari had an idea. She developed the Green Belt Movement.

What was the Green Belt Movement about? It was simple: Planting trees. Wangari wanted to bring back the green to Kenya and help women discover their power and worth. So, she reached out to women in various villages, encouraging them to do their part and plant trees.

She helped women see how, by deliberately planting trees, they'd have wood they could burn for fuel for cooking, stop soil erosion, and keep their beautiful nation from becoming nothing more than a barren desert. Wangari pulled it off. Her Green Belt Movement was so successful she and the women she connected with planted more than 30 million trees.

Like many inspirational people, Wangari didn't have it easy. Some Kenyans didn't like what she was doing. You'd think there couldn't possibly be anything offensive about planting trees, right? Think again. Kenya was in the clutches of an authoritarian, corrupt government.

The government did not like Wangari inspiring people to plant trees because what else might she encourage them to do? What if she got people to stand up against the government? So, they did everything possible to get in her way.

Wangari and those she'd recruited in the Green Belt Movement suffered constant harassment from the government, arrested, beaten to a pulp, and then thrown into jail. But this wasn't enough for the authorities because they needed to make people stop believing in the cause. This could only mean one thing.

The government figured that if they could make Wangari look bad, no one would want to be associated with her or her movement. So, what did they do? They crafted a smear campaign, using the media to churn out the most despicable of lies to get people to turn on Wangari.

When you believe in a cause and are willing to give up everything for it, nothing shakes or steers you off your path. Wangari wasn't planting trees and uplifting women for clout. She was doing it because it was a matter of life and death.

Wangari kept going, regardless of all the horrific things the media and the government cooked up to make her look like a villain. She never stopped criticizing the authorities. If anything, their cruelty and corruption encouraged her to keep going and make her voice louder than ever. She was such an inspiration and a force that even more people joined her cause.

One of the best ways to change a rotten, broken system is to join it and fix it. So, in 2002, Wangari wanted a seat in the Kenyan parliament. This way, she could use her position of power to make real changes to benefit her people. She won the seat because she had already won the hearts of most Kenyans - but that didn't mean her job would be a breeze.

It's not easy to be an environmentalist in a corrupt government that is more interested in making money than keeping the environment whole and healthy. She was always outcasted from her many opponents. Yet, she made it work. Wangari used the power and privilege of her position to make it a priority for every Kenyan to conserve the environment.

Wangari also had issues in her personal life. She was a single mother, something that was gravely frowned upon. She had to support her family while remaining focused on her cause. It's not easy to balance your attention between your goals and loved ones, but she found a way to make it work.

As if that wasn't enough to deal with, Kenya wasn't the most supportive of women who held leadership positions in those days. Wangari didn't let the negative stereotypes or opinions of others weigh her down. She never stopped fighting for what she believed in until she passed away in 2011 at age 71.

Wangari Maathai hasn't really left. You can find her in the green of over 30 million Kenyan trees and as a flame in the hearts of the millions she inspired with her courage, love for people, and concern for the environment.

Famous Quotes

1. *It's the little things citizens do. That's what will make the difference. My little thing is planting trees.*
2. *Until you dig a hole, you plant a tree, you water it, and make it survive, you haven't done a thing. You are just talking.*
3. *We need to promote development that does not destroy our environment.*
4. *We are very fond of blaming the poor for destroying the environment, but often, it is the powerful, including governments, that are responsible.*
5. *I don't really know why I care so much. I just have something inside me that tells me that there is a problem, and I have got to do something about it. I think that is what I would call the God in me.*

Chapter 8: The Greatest Sports Heroes

There are many amazing, inspiring stories of athletes who came from humble beginnings and rose to such great heights that their names will never be forgotten. The stories you discover in this chapter will inspire you to keep going and never give up on yourself. By the time you're through reading this chapter, you'll learn you have no idea how strong you are until you decide to keep going after your dreams until they become a reality, just as these athletic greats have done.

Serena Williams

There are certain people whose names everyone knows, and Serena Williams is one of them. Born in 1981 in Saginaw, Michigan, Serena Williams is a tennis player humanity will never forget. Her parents were Oracene Price and Richard Williams. Serena's mom, Oracene, was a nurse, while her father, Richard, created and managed a security service. Serena has an older sister, Venus.

Serena Williams.

Edwin Martinez, CC BY 2.0 <https://creativecommons.org/licenses/by/2.0>, via Wikimedia Commons. https://commons.wikimedia.org/wiki/File:Serena_Williams_at_2013_US_Open.jpg

Serena and Venus Williams fell in love with tennis because their father always took them to the public courts to play. Her father was a strict coach and would keep both girls practicing for long hours. Richard was so invested in his daughters' education he home-schooled them. He felt that he'd do a much better job than regular school.

Eventually, the Williams family had to move from their home in Compton, California, to West Palm Beach, Florida, when Serena was nine. This was a good move because both sisters could attend a tennis academy and improve their skills.

In 1994, Venus Williams became a professional tennis player. The year after, Serena also became a professional.

A remarkable thing about Serena's playing is how powerfully she served the ball. Her opponents knew better than to underestimate her skills, especially her groundstrokes. After so many years of hours of practice with her dad and at the tennis Academy, she became a force to be reckoned with.

Serena Williams has a way of moving on the court as if she owns it. You could think of the tennis court as her lair, and anyone daring to play against her is toast. Her playing style and athleticism soon caused many people to notice her. People were fascinated that a family had two tennis titans. Many believed Venus would be the first to bag a Grand Slam singles title. But Serena cinched it when she won the 1999 U.S. Open.

On the surface, you'd think Serena's story is a tennis fairy tale, but even fairy tales have dark, sad moments. It was the same for this amazing player. She is a Black woman in a sport where most players are White. So, when she first came onto the tennis scene, she had to deal with racism.

She was treated unfairly because she didn't fit the typical tennis player stereotype. She'd get penalized if she expressed her feelings like her male players did. This would be accepted if the men were also penalized in the same way, but they got away with it. What did she get penalized for?

During the 2018 U.S. Open final against Naomi Osaka, Serena called the umpire a thief because they had made an unfair decision against her. She was calling them out for their behavior, which male players do. Male players have said even worse things and got away with it. But Serena was punished for her outburst.

Serena received 3 penalties that day. The first was for receiving coaching, but she argued it didn't happen. The second was for smashing her racket because she was frustrated. It wasn't as if she made a habit of smashing her racket. Everyone has bad days. It's part of being human. She was going through a lot but sadly didn't receive compassion.

The third penalty was for verbal abuse because she called the umpire a liar and a thief. She wasn't proud of this moment, but, like everyone else, she made mistakes. Apart from the game and point penalties, she also had to pay $17,000 in fines. Many tennis enthusiasts considered this penalty so harsh that the whole world began discussing the double standards in tennis.

If any good came out of Serena being treated unfairly during her career, it's that her naysayers' bad behavior lit a fire in her heart to advocate for gender equality. Serena doesn't think it's fair that women don't get paid as much as men in sports. So, she speaks up for this inequality, asking for it to be fixed.

Serena has suffered many injuries throughout her career, sometimes so bad she's had to take a break from playing tennis altogether. For three years, between 2004 and 2006, she suffered severe injuries to her knees. It was a dark time for her because she was suddenly no longer a top 100 tennis player.

In 2011, a life-threatening incident happened to Serena. She had a pulmonary embolism. A blood clot blocked one or more arteries in her lungs. As if that wasn't enough, in 2016, she couldn't participate in tournaments because her knee and shoulder were badly inflamed. Four years later, in 2020, she had an Achilles tendon injury, forcing her to end her season earlier.

In her personal life, she dealt with setbacks and challenges. In 2017, she gave birth to a beautiful baby girl. Unfortunately, she couldn't be as present with her baby as she wanted because she had postpartum depression, a mental condition of new mothers where they are unable to find joy in anything after giving birth. The birth was not smooth, as she had to have emergency cesarean surgery. Additionally, more blood clots appeared in her lungs, which meant she needed another surgery.

Serena isn't only about tennis. Not only does she speak up for equal pay, but she also raises awareness of the alarming death rate affecting White mothers. Using her privilege and wealth, she gives marginalized female business owners a chance to hold their heads high by offering them whatever they need to succeed. If there's one thing this legendary tennis player has always been passionate about, it is women's rights.

Serena Williams has dedicated her life to finding the barriers that hold people back from achieving greatness and breaking them. She knows what it's like to be stereotyped and kept from opportunities because of people's unfair opinions. So, she has committed all her resources to resolving these problems.

Her story is a reminder that because things have always been a certain way, it doesn't mean they can't change for the better. Despite the obstacles and problems she faced in her professional and personal life, she continues to inspire many with her perseverance and dedication to her causes.

Famous Quotes

1. *I don't like to lose - at anything - yet I've grown most not from victories but setbacks.*
2. *If Plan A isn't working, I have Plan B, Plan C, and even Plan D.*
3. *If I don't get it right, I won't stop until I do.*
4. *Luck has nothing to do with it. I have spent many, many hours, countless hours on the court working for my one moment in time, not knowing when it would come.*
5. *If winning is God's reward, then losing is how he teaches us.*

Lionel Messi

Lionel Messi was born in 1987 into a working-class family in Rosario, Argentina. His mother worked as a cleaner, while his father was a factory steel worker. His passion for football began when he was very young. It was obvious to anyone watching him play soccer with his older brothers and cousins that he had what it would take to become one of the greats if he kept up his practice.

Lionel Messi.

Tasnim News Agency, CC BY 4.0 <https://creativecommons.org/licenses/by/4.0>, via Wikimedia Commons. https://commons.wikimedia.org/wiki/File:Lionel_Messi_WC2022.jpg

When he was only four years old, Lionel joined the Grandoli local football club, where his father was his coach. Lionel would practice his skills daily, and his grandmother would watch him, cheering him on. At age eight, Lionel joined the Newell Old Boys, a football club in his native Rosario. It was a dream come true for him because he had always looked up to the players in that club. At this point, it was pretty obvious what his career would be. Lionel lived and breathed football.

Lionel lost his grandmother when he was only ten. This loss rocked the family to their core and broke the young boy. She was his biggest fan, and he couldn't comprehend that he'd never see her again. He was so heartbroken he refused to touch a football for weeks. However, his dad encouraged him to keep on going. He told him to play for the club, so Lionel found a bit of his spark again, playing nonstop.

The older Lionel got, the more concerned his parents were because he was not growing taller. At eleven, they took him to a doctor. They learned the horrible news that Lionel had a growth hormone deficiency. The only way he'd ever grow was if he underwent specific treatment, which would cost them $1500 every month for the next three years. Sadly, Lionel's parents couldn't afford it. Lionel's dad did the only thing he could think of. He reached out to Newell's Old Boys Club to help them financially.

Lionel Messi and his family moved to Barcelona when he was thirteen, and he played for FC Barcelona's Under 14 team. Thankfully, his new football club was happy to sponsor Lionel's treatment. During his time with the football club, he scored 21 goals in 14 games for the junior team. A rising star, he rapidly moved through the ranks, playing for higher-level teams until he was sixteen, when he informally debuted with FC Barcelona in a friendly game.

Lionel Messi became the youngest-ever official player and goal scorer in the Spanish La Liga at age 17. He wasn't the tallest footballer in the world. He was only 5 foot 7 and weighed 148 lbs., but he was powerful, strong, and had great balance. It also helped that he was very flexible on the football field, switching from defense to attack as needed.

Few players know how to control the ball as quickly and precisely as Lionel does. Favoring his left foot, there is no defense tightly packed enough to keep him from passing the ball where he wants it to go. His skills are so awesome that people compare him to Pele or Diego Maradona.

The problem with being so skilled at something is people expect you always to get it right. Messi's country, club, and fans expected him to continue scoring goals, breaking records, and winning trophies. Looking at Messi's career, he hasn't disappointed, but that's a lot of pressure for one person to carry. Yet he managed to pull it off.

Rivals, critics, and the media often scrutinized everything he did. Whenever he failed or made a mistake, they criticized him as though he had never done anything great. So, he put pressure on himself because he wanted to keep improving and achieving greater goals.

Despite this pressure and other problems such as tax issues, controversies, and personal problems, Messi kept his head held high, even today. His playing style was so unique that every footballer worldwide picked up a trick or two from him.

Lionel Messi's story is inspirational because he made it from a small town in Argentina onto the global map, cementing his place in history as one of the greatest footballers of all time. He's such a great guy that he's also a philanthropist. He established the Leo Messi Foundation to help children access health care and education. His focus is on children who have been victims of violence, war, poverty, disabilities, and illnesses.

Famous Quotes

1. *When you lose, you get up, you make mistakes, and you learn. And then you become a better player.*
2. *You can overcome anything if and only if you love something enough.*
3. *It took me 17 years and 114 days to become an overnight success.*
4. *The day you think there are no improvements to be made is a sad one for any player.*
5. *You have to fight to reach your dream. You have to sacrifice and work hard for it.*

Michael Jordan

Michael Jordan was born in Brooklyn, New York, in 1963, but his family moved to Wilmington, North Carolina. His parents were Deloris and James R. Jordan, Sr. His father worked as an equipment supervisor, while his mother was a bank employee. Michael had an older sister, Deloris, two older brothers, Larry Jordan and James R. Jordan Jr, and a younger sister, Roslyn.

Michael Jordan.

Steve Lipofsky Basketballphoto.com, CC BY-SA 3.0 <https://creativecommons.org/licenses/by-sa/3.0>, via Wikimedia Commons.

https://commons.wikimedia.org/wiki/File:Jordan_Lipofsky.jpg

At Wilmington, Michael went to Emsley A. Laney High School, where he showed off his athletic skills in football, baseball, and basketball. Michael had always loved sports but didn't make the cut when he tried out for his high school basketball team as a sophomore. So, he played for junior varsity instead. The only reason he wasn't chosen for the team was because, at 5 foot 11, he wasn't tall enough for that level. He felt terrible because, in his heart, he believed he could do much better than the players who made the team. Others may have given up at this point, but not Michael. He let his sadness and disappointment motivate him to do better.

Michael's hard work eventually paid off. He became the star player of the junior varsity team at Laney, racking up games with as many as 40 points. Thankfully, over the next summer, he gained an extra 4 inches or 10 centimeters in height. Not only did he grow taller, but he also became more skilled because he trained long and hard to improve in every way possible.

Eventually, Michael made it onto the varsity roster. During the last two seasons of his high school games, he scored at least 25 points per game. He was chosen to play for a team in the 1981 McDonald's All-American Game. Whoever decided to take him on must have been happy because he scored 30 points. His average points per game then was 27, his average rebounds per game was 12, and he averaged six assists per game that season.

Long story short, Michael caught the eye of every recruiter. He played for various college basketball programs, including North Carolina, South Carolina, Duke, Syracuse, and Virginia. He got a basketball scholarship to the University of North Carolina at Chapel Hill in 1981. He studied cultural geography because it was connected to meteorology, a subject that interested him. Michael once thought he'd have a career as a meteorologist. If only he knew the path life would take him. At North Carolina, Michael played under the watchful eye of coach Dean Smith, a legend in his own right.

Michael Jordan's performance was so phenomenal that he would be called Atlantic Coast Conference Rookie of the Year in his first season. Without him, his team might not have secured the national championship. It would have gone to Georgetown instead. Throughout his sophomore and junior years, Michael continued to stun many basketball enthusiasts, breaking records and winning awards.

In 1984, Michael left college after his junior year and entered the NBA draft. He joined the Chicago Bulls as the team's third pick, and it didn't take long for Michael Jordan to take the NBA by storm. He gained a massive number of fans who were amazed at his skills. Michael Jordan, or "MJ," won the Rookie of the Year award and was chosen for the All-Star team in his first season.

This famous basketball player set so many incredible records that it would take a few more chapters to get it all down. In 1986, he was in a playoff game against the Boston Celtics, scoring 63 points, the highest points ever scored in a playoff game. Besides Wilt Chamberlain, MJ was the only player to score a whopping 3000 points in one season from 1986 to 1987.

In 1998, MJ was named Defensive Player of the Year. In 1988, 1991, 1992, 1996, and 1998, MJ was the NBA's Most Valuable Player.

After he led the Chicago Bulls to the championship three times in a row, MJ lost his father in 1993 to a robbery. He was so devastated he briefly retired from basketball. He thought he'd try his hand at baseball. Still, he returned to basketball two years after his retirement in 1995 and kept winning championship after championship. After he played the 1997 to 1998 season, he retired.

For Michael Jordan, retiring didn't mean he was completely done with basketball. In January 2000, he bought a share of the Washington Wizards and became the team's president of basketball operations. MJ was about more than just sitting behind desks and figuring out rosters. In September 2001, he pulled out of owning and managing the Washington Wizards, choosing to become a player on the team instead. The NBA was more than happy to have him back since people were no longer as interested in the league since he retired.

Michael Jordan gave it one more shot with his final 2002 to 2003 season. By the end of his career, he had 32,292 points and a 30.12 points per game average, which no one else in the league's history has ever done. He also had 2,514 steals over his career, the second-most steals in history.

As usual, MJ found a way to stay close to the sport even in this last retirement. He became a minority owner of the NBA's Charlotte Bobcats, renamed the Charlotte Hornets. He bought a larger share of the team in 2010, making him the first former NBA player who owned a major part of a franchise in the league.

Michael Jordan's height was an advantage to his career at a whopping 6 ft. 6, equivalent to 1.98 meters. His ability to shoot, pass, and defend the ball is so impressive people called him Air Jordan since he could leap so high into the air that it seemed he was flying or floating. While in the air, he made his body move incredibly. Michael never had issues with money because he received millions of dollars thanks to endorsements. He also got a nice chunk of change from his Air Jordan basketball shoes.

In 1996, Michael Jordan dabbled into live-action and animation films by releasing a movie titled Space Jam. He was the star of this movie alongside the famous Looney Tunes animated characters Daffy Duck and Bugs Bunny. The movie did incredibly well. He was inducted into the Naismith Memorial Basketball Hall of Fame in 2009. In 2016, Michael Jordan was awarded the Presidential Medal of Freedom.

Michael Jordan had challenges, too. In his second season, he broke a foot and had to sit out 64 games. For someone so passionate about basketball, you can only imagine how heartbreaking it was to not participate in games or play with his teammates.

In 1989, he injured his back, and in 1995 he suffered a wrist injury. You need time to recuperate when you're a basketballer and get hurt. The problem is, when you heal, you must work hard to get back to playing as well as you did before your injury. MJ had to put in extra time to recover his original fitness and form. Add the pressure of people always expecting him to win, and you'll understand how hard it must have been for him.

No matter what life threw at Michael Jordan, he could bounce back. His truly resilient spirit was why he became the greatest basketball player in history. By following his passion, he became an icon who continues to inspire millions of people around the world.

Famous Quotes

1. *Just play. Have fun. Enjoy the game.*
2. *My attitude is that if you push me towards something that you think is a weakness, then I will turn that perceived weakness into a strength.*
3. *There is no I in "team," but there is in "win."*
4. *I failed over and over and over again in my life and that is why I succeed.*
5. *Some people want it to happen, some wish it would happen, others make it happen.*

Usain Bolt

Born in 1986 in Sherwood Content, Jamaica, Usain Bolt is a living legend. He spent his childhood days with his parents, brother, and sister. His mom and dad ran a grocery store. As a child, Usain Bolt was fascinated by football and cricket. In school, coaches noticed that he was fast and incredibly agile. So, they gave him a little nudge to try track and field. Much to his delight, Usain realized he was a natural sprinter and soon competed in events locally and across the country.

Usain Bolt.

Erik van Leeuwen (GFDL <http://www.gnu.org/copyleft/fdl.html> or GFDL <http://www.gnu.org/copyleft/fdl.html>), via Wikimedia Commons. https://commons.wikimedia.org/wiki/File:Usain_Bolt_smiling_Berlin_2009.JPG

Usain permanently stamped his name on the history books when he was fifteen. He became the youngest World Junior champion in the 200m race, finishing at a record time of 20.61 seconds. He bagged himself the gold medal in Kingston, Jamaica! The media gave him a new nickname: Lightning Bolt. And, just like that, he became a national sensation. After this, he won two silver medals in the 4 x 100 and 4 x 400 meters relay races.

Things weren't always easy for Usain. Competitive running can take its toll on the body, and Bolt had to struggle with injuries to his hamstrings, making it difficult to train or run. In 2010, he had a back injury so terrible he had to undergo surgery, which meant he couldn't compete for the rest of the season. In 2014, he hurt his foot, requiring surgery, which meant he couldn't run for months. He almost didn't participate in the Rio competition in 2016 because of his injured hamstring. Still, he recovered in time for the competition. In 2017, he had another hamstring injury at the London World Championships, causing him to wrap up his career in pain.

In 2008, Usain Bolt shocked the world by breaking records in the 100 and 200-meter races. This monumental event happened at the Beijing Olympics. The whole world watched in wonder at the style and speed with which Usain ran. At this event, he gave his signature pose for the first time. Usain Bolt became the first male athlete to win both races and set world record times. He broke the records at the same Olympic event, making it an even more celebrated event. It was a unicorn moment, yet Usain Bolt made the impossible not just possible but real. He cemented his position as the fastest man in the world. Millions fell in love with him for his skill and because he was such an easy-going, charismatic, and joyful person.

For the next 8 years, Usain Bolt kept sprinting his heart out. He secured 6 gold medals from the Olympics in London in 2012 and Rio in 2016. Do you have any idea how impossible it seemed to win the 100 and 200m titles three times in a row at three different Olympics? No one could have seen it happen. No one could have expected it because if you'd asked anyone before Usain Bolt, they'd tell you it was impossible. But he made it happen.

Usain Bolt is such a phenomenal sprinter that he went on to win 11 world championship gold medals. He would break his record again before his rival sprinters could match his most recent speed. He was always several meters ahead of the pack. Sure, some people gave him a run for his money, like Justin Gatlin and Tyson Gay, but he always left them eating his dust. Usain Bolt's records and story inspired young athletes all over the world, and they wanted to be just like him.

In 2017, Bolt retired from athletics. He wasn't happy with his performance at the World Championships in London. He didn't rake in a gold or silver medal but placed third in the 100-meter race. As for the 4 x 400-meter relay, he hurt himself during the race. It was heartbreaking, but he knew it was time to say goodbye to his fans and the sport he loved. Usain knew he'd had a good run, so he was satisfied with his career and didn't regret anything. In his words, he had accomplished everything he desired. How many people get to say that?

Famous Quotes

1. *There are better starters than me, but I am a strong finisher.*
2. *I don't think limits.*
3. *A lot of legends and a lot of people have come before me. But this is my time.*

4. *I know what I can do, so it doesn't bother me what other people think or their opinions on the situation.*
5. *When you're running, if you see you're going to win, you're going to celebrate.*

Bebe Vio

Beatrice Maria Adelaide Marzia Vio is nothing short of a living legend. Also known as Bebe Vio, she was born in Venice, Italy, in 1997, as the second child of three. She grew up in the town of Mogliano Veneto in northeastern Italy. Her story is a reminder that no matter what terrible things you experience, you can turn them around for good. With the right spirit, you can take a bad situation and make it the best thing ever to happen to you.

Bebe Vio.

© Marie-Lan Nguyen / Wikimedia Commons.

https://commons.wikimedia.org/wiki/File:Bebe_Vio_2014_IWAS_European_Championships_FFS-IN_t173213.jpg

Bebe has loved fencing since she was a young child. It all started when she was five years old, and since then, she hasn't been able to give it up. When she was eleven, things took a turn for the worse. She had *meningitis*, a serious and sometimes fatal illness.

Your brain and spinal cord are kept safe by a covering called *meninges*. When viruses, bacteria, or fungi infect this covering, it becomes a serious condition. If it's not treated right away, it can worsen in a matter of hours.

With Bebe, her meningitis was so bad it made it difficult for her blood to move around her body properly, causing sepsis. The sepsis meant her body was fighting so hard to take down the germs causing meningitis that it attacked healthy organs, too, causing her to be terribly inflamed.

Her life was at risk, and there was only one way to save it. She had to have her limbs amputated - both legs cut off at the knee and both forearms removed. This happened late in 2008. Can you imagine how she must have felt, knowing she might never fence again?

Bebe is no ordinary person. It would take a lot more than losing her limbs to make her give up. It took three months of hard work and intense rehab after her amputation, but soon, she was ready to return to fencing. This time, she fenced using a wheelchair and prosthetics. She may not have had arms, but she realized she could use her shoulder just as well to enjoy the game.

She also had great parents, Ruggero and Teresa Vio, who encouraged her to get back to fencing. Her father found the best specialists who could craft prosthetic limbs to suit Bebe so she could fence by holding her foil with her shoulder.

Federica Berton and Alice Esposito coached Bebe, so she was in good hands, and her skills improved massively. The first time she competed in a wheelchair fencing competition was in 2010. Bebe was such an inspiration to her parents that they set up Art4sport Onlus. This non-profit organization helps young amputees who have athletic hopes and dreams.

At the 2012 Summer Paralympics, Bebe's career was still fresh, so she couldn't be a part of it, at least not by fencing. She was given the honor of torchbearer for the event's opening after over 1,000 people emailed the International Paralympic Committee to consider her for the job.

Bebe became world famous when she bagged her first-ever World Cup in 2013 in Montreal. Her opponent was Gyöngyi Dani, who won an Olympic silver medal. Bebe's performance was so impressive that the International Paralympic Committee named her the Paralympic Athlete of the Month.

In the 2013 - 14 season, Bebe decided to give her fencing a break because she wanted to study. She couldn't stay away for too long, though, so she went back to fencing and competing in June 2014 and won the team and individual competition at the European Championships. When the year ended, the Italian Paralympics Committee honored her with the title of the Italian Paralympic Athlete of the Year, which she shared with another amazing athlete, Oxana Corso.

In 2015, she went up against Gyöngyi Dani again. She defeated her opponent 15 - 4 in the final competition, making her the world champion. In that same year, the Milan Expo 2015 made her an ambassador. She also published her autobiography, titled Mi Hanno Regalato un Sogno, "They Gave Me a Dream."

Bebe was given the Mangiarotti Award in the 2015 - 16 season by the Italian Olympic Committee. After that, she secured another gold medal in the Rio 2016 Paralympic Games, where she battled Zhou Jingjing from China. If the world didn't know who Bebe was before this event, they certainly did when she was done. The media couldn't get enough of her, and for good reason. Her story is an inspiration to millions.

In 2023, Bebe Vio graduated from John Cabot University, Rome, with a Communication and International Relations degree. She loved fencing, but that meant she gave up on her education because fencing mattered just as much to her. Let her story inspire you to make your unique problems and challenges work in your favor!

Famous Quotes

1. *I promise: all you have is everything you need.*
2. *Isn't it possible? I'm sorry, I don't understand those words.*
3. *If you are not the one who decides you want to live well, you will never do it.*
4. *My motto is "Life is too good."*
5. *If it seems impossible, then it can be done!*

Chapter 9: Heroes in the Shadows – 3 Unrecognized Legends

When it comes to history, there are so many things and legends to cover that some people get forgotten, even if they've done the most astounding work. In this chapter, you will read about 3 heroes who have remained in the shadows, unrecognized by the modern world for the most part.

You're about to discover how these three incredible people changed the world and made it better. When you've read their stories, you may feel the desire to whisper a "thank you" because the world wouldn't be as awesome as it is without their contributions.

Alan Turing

Also known as the father of modern computer science, Alan Turing was an extraordinary person who lived a challenging life. He was born in London, England, in 1912. From a very young age, he was clearly in love with science and mathematics, wanting to know everything about those topics. He wasn't just interested in mathematics. He was also a math whiz.

Alan Turning.

https://commons.wikimedia.org/wiki/File:Alan_Turing_(1912-1954)_in_1936_at_Princeton_University.jpg

Alan's love for mathematics pushed him to study it at the University of Cambridge, where he achieved excellent work on probability theory.

But he wasn't your average student.

The ideas that came out of his mind were simply astonishing; without them, computer science wouldn't be a thing. His Turing machine was one of the greatest ideas he shared with the world. It did not exist then, but he thought it was possible to make; he already understood how and why *modern computers* work the way they do!

Turing got a Ph.D. from Princeton University in 1938. He'd been learning a lot under the watch of Alonzo Church, a brilliant mathematician. In World War II, Alan had to work at Bletchley Park with the Government Code and Cyber School. The Germans had a special piece of technology called the Enigma machine, which they used to relay important messages back and forth. If Britain could crack the code, they'd have valuable information to help them win the war.

If you had asked people then, they'd have told you it was impossible to break the Enigma code. It was Turing who helped the government get past the so-called unbreakable encryption. He created an electromechanical machine, which he named "bombe," to pull off the impossible, and this was how he helped the Allies during the war.

Unfortunately, Alan was born at a time when people were very judgmental. It didn't matter to them that he had done so much for the war and to advance computer science. Why? People didn't like him because of his sexuality. It was illegal to be a homosexual in the United Kingdom. So, in 1952, he was convicted of what they called "gross indecency." Imagine being convicted because you are in love with someone.

The government gave Alan two options. They would either throw him in jail or give him hormonal treatment that would stop him from wanting to be with anyone. It was like being stuck between a rock and a hard place. Alan chose the hard place. As you can probably imagine, this was a terrible thing for his emotional and physical health.

In 1954, Alan died from cyanide poisoning. His body was found in bed. Some think he was murdered, while others assumed he was so miserable from the chemical treatment the government gave him that he decided to take his own life. While he met a sad and tragic end, Alan Turing's legacy lives on, especially in artificial intelligence and computer science.

Famous Quotes

1. *We can only see a short distance ahead, but we can see plenty there that needs to be done.*
2. *Sometimes, it is the people no one can imagine anything of who do the things no one can imagine.*
3. *Those who can imagine anything can create the impossible.*
4. *One day, ladies will take their computers for walks in the park and tell each other, "My little computer said such a funny thing this morning."*
5. *We like to believe that man is, in some subtle way, superior to the rest of creation.*

Rosalind Franklin

Born in 1920 in London, England, Rosalind Franklin was always a bright student deeply interested in science. She went to Saint Paul's Girls School, and from there, she went to Newnham College, University of Cambridge, to study physical chemistry.

Rosalind Franklin.

CSHL, derivative work Lämpel, CC BY-SA 4.0 <https://creativecommons.org/licenses/by-sa/4.0>, via Wikimedia Commons. https://commons.wikimedia.org/wiki/File:Rosalind-franklin-in-paris_crop.jpg

During World War II, Franklin worked as a London Air Raid warden. The British Coal Utilization Research Association employed her to study coal and carbon to understand their physical chemistry. She learned so much from her research that she eventually wrote her doctoral thesis on it. Cambridge thought it was good enough to give her a doctorate in 1945.

When the war was over, Rosalind packed her bags and moved to France. She went to the State Chemical Laboratory and partnered with Jacques Méring. She was interested in X-ray diffraction tech, which would shape her work in the future.

In 1951, Rosalind became part of King's College's Biophysical Laboratory in London, where she'd use what she learned about X-ray diffraction to study DNA. There wasn't much information on what DNA looked like back then. Still, thanks to Rosalind's passion and dedication, she discovered much that would change the world, including the discovery that DNA is structured like a helix and has a high density.

Thanks to Rosalind's work, Francis Crick and James Watson figured out in 1953 that DNA was a double-helix polymer. They proposed it was a spiral of two strands of DNA wrapped around each other. They'd never have known this if Rosalind hadn't done the groundwork.

It wasn't easy being Rosalind. She was in a field that was mainly more men than women. Back then, men thought women weren't as bright or capable as they were. Even when women came up with excellent theories, concepts, solutions, or inventions, the men would dismiss them. When they did realize these ideas were pretty good, they wouldn't admit it. It was hard for the men to credit women for their brilliant minds and hard work. Rosalind suffered from this discrimination every day. Still, she didn't let it stop her from continuing her scientific work.

Tragedy struck Rosalind in 1956 when she noticed her clothes no longer fit, and it wasn't because she suddenly had such a big appetite that she ate for two. She went back to London and discovered the reason for her weight gain. She had ovarian cancer. She battled with this disease for two more years before she died in 1958.

Famous Quotes

1. *Science and everyday life cannot and should not be separated.*
2. *Science, for me, gives me a partial explanation for life. In so far as it goes, it is based on fact, experience, and experiment.*
3. *In my view, all that is necessary for faith is the belief that by doing our best, we shall succeed in our aims: the improvement of mankind.*
4. *What's the use of doing all this work if we don't get some fun out of this?*
5. *Your faith rests on the future of yourself and others as individuals, mine in the future, and the fate of our successors. It seems to me that yours is the more selfish.*

Bayard Rustin

Bayard Rustin is another unsung hero who deserves to be remembered. He was born in West Chester, Pennsylvania, in 1912 to a family of Quakers who believe there's nothing more important than being good to others and maintaining peace in every way. These were the values that Bayard and his family lived by. His family also did what they could to support the civil rights movement.

Bayard Rustin.

https://commons.wikimedia.org/wiki/File:BayardRustinAug1963-LibraryOfCongress_crop.jpg

Bayard had always been smart, so it's no surprise he went to Wilberforce University, Cheney State Teachers College, and City College of New York. He loved to know and learn and never assumed he knew it all. His mind was like a sponge, soaking up everything it could.

Those who knew Bayard in person would have told you he was very good with people. He had charisma, which meant he could make you feel good without trying too hard if you hung out with him. People also found him interesting because he made money as a singer when he was in New York. He sang spiritual songs in clubs, and his performances were loved.

The fight for civil rights was near and dear to Bayard's heart, so even as a grown-up, he kept going. His passion didn't go unnoticed, and soon, he worked alongside prominent leaders of the civil rights movement like James Farmer, A. Philip Randolph, and the legendary Martin Luther King Jr. As awesome as his work was, it wasn't enough for some people, who hated his race and hated his sexual orientation even more.

Being openly gay in Rustin's time could get you into a lot of trouble. So, he was arrested in 1953 and spent 50 nights in jail. It was a cruel time to love who you wanted to love in those days. Since everyone knew he was gay, Rustin preferred to continue his work behind the scenes rather than take on a prominent role in the civil rights movement.

At some point in the 50s, Rustin became Martin Luther King Jr.'s close adviser. Knowing what Martin stood for and hoped to achieve was an honorable position. Bayard also worked with the King's Southern Christian Leadership Conference as the principal organizer. Later, in August 1963, there was a March on Washington to show support for laws that would make civil rights legal and real in America. The march's architect was none other than Bayard Rustin.

A year after the march, Bayard rallied students across New York City from public schools to boycott school for a day. He didn't do it for fun. The boycott was to voice their anger and pain at the racial injustice and imbalance in the school system. After this boycott, Bayard became the president of the A. Philip Randolph Institute, which was committed to the civil rights cause. He remained with the institute from 1966 to 1979.

Bayard reached a point in his life where he realized there was another fight he had to become a part of. He was tired of living in the shadows, feeling like a criminal because people didn't think he and others like him should be allowed to love who their hearts wanted. He was tired of people acting like he chose his sexual orientation or thinking he could and should switch it off. But he chose not to. He was tired of being invalidated.

So, in the 80s, Bayard spoke up for gay rights. The movement was already in place, but it was tough going. Since he already had experience as an activist working for the civil rights movement, he applied what he knew to solve the problem of discrimination against gay people. One of the most remarkable things he did was testify in favor of the Gay Rights Bill of New York in 1986.

Bayard wanted much more than for it to stop being a legal crime to be gay. He also wanted to change how society treated homosexual people because he knew that was where the true victory would be in the fight for gay rights, a battle for the right of humans to live freely and with dignity. He did so much for both movements he was passionate about but rarely got the credit for his work. Some people didn't like that he was once connected to the Communist Party, and others didn't like that he was gay.

Yet, despite the lack of recognition, Bayard kept on trucking. He was an activist until the very end, when he died in 1987. Only after his death did people realize his worth and appreciate his contributions to society. In 2013, he was given a posthumous award: The Presidential Medal of Freedom. In 2020, Bayard was posthumously pardoned for the unfair conviction he received in 1953.

Sure, he's long gone and may not care about these things, but it's nice to know that he touched society so deeply that it's now recognizing how hard he worked to make the world a free, fair, and inclusive place. If you could ask him, he'd probably tell you he sees this as progress, but there's still a lot of work to be done.

Famous Quotes

1. *People will never fight for your freedom if you have not given evidence that you are prepared to fight for it yourself.*
2. *We need, in every community, a group of angelic troublemakers.*
3. *When an individual is protesting society's refusal to acknowledge his dignity as a human being, his very act of protest confers dignity on him.*
4. *There are three ways in which one can deal with an injustice. (a) One can accept it without protest. (b) One can seek to avoid it. (c) One can resist the injustice non-violently. To accept it is to perpetuate it.*
5. *We are all one – and if we don't know it, we will learn it the hard way.*

Chapter 10: Exhilarating Explorers

There's no better way to bring this book to a close than by ending on an exhilarating high. The stories you're about to discover are about people who weren't afraid to explore the world. They were brave, going where no one else dared. You'll read how they changed the world in their own way and be fired up to get started on whatever burning desires you have in your heart.

Amelia Earheart

Amelia Mary Earhart was born in Atchison, Kansas, in 1897. She was not your average little girl because it was obvious to everyone that she loved adventures. She'd rather do her own thing because she wanted to, not because she was told to. This daring, courageous spirit never left her. She was a naturally curious person and allowed her interests to take her wherever they led.

Amelia Earhart.

https://commons.wikimedia.org/wiki/File:Amelia_Earhart_standing_under_nose_of_her_Lockheed_Model_10-E_Electra,_small.jpg

After high school in 1916 in Chicago, she enrolled at the Ogontz School in Rydal, Pennsylvania. But she wasn't there for as long as she'd thought she'd be. She'd grown interested in caring for the wounded and sick soldiers in World War 1. She wanted to help, so she left junior college, packed up her things, and went to Toronto to serve as a nurse's aide.

When the war was over, Amelia went to New York City. There, she entered Columbia University's premed program. Her stay there didn't last long either. Her parents preferred that she live as close to them as possible, and she was okay with that. So, in 1920, she left New York City and went to California. Here, she'd ride an airplane for the first time. And once she did, she was hooked. She immediately took flying lessons.

Amelia bought her first plane in 1921 – which was a big deal. It was a Kinner Airster. In 1923, she got her pilot's license, which meant she could take to the skies whenever she pleased. In the middle of the 1920s, she packed up her things and headed to Massachusetts to become a social worker. She worked at the Denison House, where immigrants in Boston could settle down and figure out their lives.

Amelia's change in plans didn't mean she'd fallen out of love with her plane and the skies. She was still passionate about flying. Following her heart, she became the first female passenger to fly across the Atlantic in an airplane. The pilot on this flight was Wilmer Stultz. It wasn't common to have women flying back then. Amelia instantly became a celebrity when word got around about her achievement.

You don't work hard to get a pilot's license just to settle for being a passenger. That wasn't Amelia's dream. She wanted to pilot an actual flight. She wanted to be the person in the cockpit of a plane.

Since Amelia always did what her heart wanted, she made it happen. In 1932, she flew a transatlantic flight on her own with no copilot. The aircraft was a Lockheed Vega 5B with no stops. Once more, she was the first woman to pull this off. She was awarded the United States Distinguished Flying Cross for her incredible achievement.

Amelia Earhart did all she could to give women more opportunities to work in the aviation industry. She was on fire, setting record after record. Did you know she's the first woman to fly on her own at a height above 14,000 feet? She's also the main reason The Ninety-Nines was formed, an organization specifically for female pilots.

As with every other great person, Earhart had to face challenges. The aviation industry was mostly men. The typical attitude of most men toward women then wasn't great. They didn't know what to do with Amelia, a woman interested in being a pilot. They doubted her, but she didn't let that bother her. She went after her dreams, which made her an icon many admired and are still inspired by today.

One of the most daring things Amelia attempted was a flight around the world in 1937. She wanted to be the first woman in history to finish this flight. She went with her navigator, Fred Noonan. Sadly, once they were flying over the central Pacific Ocean, they disappeared close to Howland Island.

Great efforts were made to find Amelia, Fred, and their plane, but with no luck. People assumed her aircraft had run out of fuel. A 2017 documentary on the History Channel suggested Amelia and Fred survived the crash, landing in the Marshall Islands only to be captured by the Japanese. The documentary also speculates on the US government's knowledge about what really happened all this time.

In 2024, researchers claimed to have found the missing plane using advanced technology. She flew a Lockheed 10-E Electra on this final, fateful flight. Before this discovery in 2024, some bones were found on a Pacific Island (around 1938). In 2018, forensic analysis revealed that those bones were Amelia's.

Amelia Earhart will always be remembered for her resilience and determination. She was a courageous person, and because she dared to explore the skies, she gave wings to other women who, once upon a time, could only dream of flying.

Famous Quotes

1. *The most difficult thing is the decision to act. The rest is merely tenacity. The fears are paper tigers. You can do anything you decide to do. You can act to change and control your life, and the procedure, the process, is its own reward.*
2. *The most effective way to do it is to do it.*
3. *Women, like men, should try to do the impossible, and when they fail, their failure should be a challenge to others.*
4. *Never interrupt someone doing what you said couldn't be done.*
5. *Adventure is worthwhile in itself.*

Neil Armstrong

Neil Alden Armstrong was born in Wapakoneta, Ohio, in 1930. The first time he got on a plane, he was only 6 years old. Right then, he discovered his passion for airplanes and flying. Ten years later, in 1946, at just sixteen years old, he got his pilot's license. You could say that was the best birthday gift he'd ever gotten. In 1947, he became a naval air cadet.

Neil Armstrong.

https://commons.wikimedia.org/wiki/File:Neil_Armstrong_pose.jpg

Neil had been studying at Purdue University, learning about aeronautical engineering, but he didn't finish his studies. In 1950, he had to serve in the Korean War. This was a scary time for him, but he showed up and did what his country needed. He was even shot down, and fortunately for the world, he survived. He was awarded three Air Medals for his bravery.

Neil finally wrapped up his studies in 1955, bagging his degree. With no time to lose, he immediately began working with the National Advisory Committee for Aeronautics (NACA), which would eventually become the National Aeronautics and Space Administration, or NASA as everyone calls it. He was a civilian research pilot and spent over 1,100 hours in the air. But he wasn't just flying. His work was to test the performance of fighter planes. He also worked on the X-15 rocket plane.

Neil decided to be part of the space program in 1962. He wanted to be part of the NASA Astronaut Corps - and succeeded - making it into the second group of astronauts chosen in 1962. In 1966, he was the command pilot of the spacecraft Gemini 8. He and fellow astronaut David R. Scott met up with an empty, unmanned spacecraft known as the Agena rocket. It was the first time that two spacecraft would be docked or joined together in space.

Once the docking was complete, there was trouble. The rocket thruster on their spacecraft developed problems, a horrible thing to experience when you're out in space because it's the thruster that helps the craft switch directions and move.

The Gemini 8 had a thruster that fired when it shouldn't have. So, their spacecraft spun uncontrollably. They had no choice but to undock their craft from the Agena. Afterward, Neil regained complete control of the Gemini 8 and had to land the craft immediately. It was an emergency splashdown landing in the Pacific Ocean.

NASA's Apollo program from the 60s and 70s was meant to put someone on the moon. The US wanted to beat Russia to it. On May 25, 1961, the president of the US, John F. Kennedy, set the goal to not only land a manned craft on the moon but return to Earth, too.

Finally, in 1969, 8 years later, Commander Neil Armstrong, Command Module Pilot Michael Collins, and Lunar Module Pilot Edwin "Buzz" Aldrin, Jr. went on the Apollo 11 mission. The Apollo 11 craft was launched from Cape Kennedy on July 16 that year, with at least 650 million people watching on television.

Four days after they blasted off, on July 20, the team landed on the moon at 4:17 PM, US Eastern Daylight Time. Neil expertly guided the lunar landing module, touching down close to the Sea of Tranquility, or Mare Tranquillitatis, near the southwestern part. This area is large and dark, a plain you can see from Earth. It was given its name by astronomers Francesco Grimaldi and Giovanni Battista Riccioli in 1651 because it's so flat and smooth that it looks like a calm ocean.

The world watched Neil as he stepped foot on the dusty moon and heard him describe the mission as "one small step for [a] man, one giant leap for mankind." Neil and Edwin took pictures, collected samples, and set up their scientific equipment. Michael Collins remained in the Columbia - the space command module, not the country - while Neil and Buzz landed on the moon in Eagle, the name of the Lunar Module.

The US won the Space Race, and President John F. Kennedy's goal was accomplished in time. He'd wanted this to happen before the decade ended, and it did.

Some naysayers believe the moon landing was faked, but it isn't true. Beaming TV signals from the moon's orbit to the Earth wasn't new, as it had been done way before the Apollo 11 mission, using a technique called Earth-Moon-Earth communication, known as "moon bounce." Technology had definitely improved by the time Neil visited the moon.

Two hundred and forty thousand miles away from the moon, millions had to see this stellar moment to believe it. Otherwise, convincing them that the US had put someone on the moon would have been hard. The timing of the moon landing was perfect because America had had a rough decade: the Vietnam War, recovering from Kennedy's assassination and dealing with opposition to much-needed civil rights. So, with Apollo 11 touching down on the moon's surface, America reminded the world why it's such a great nation - and it's all thanks to the courage of Neil Armstrong and his team.

After Neil and Buzz spent 21 hours and 36 minutes on the magnificent moon, it was time for them to return to Earth. So, they wrapped up their work, left the moon's surface in the Eagle, and met up with Collins in the Columbia before heading back to Earth. If you're wondering why people talk about Neil more than they do Buzz, it's because he was the first to set foot on the moon.

The crew executed a splashdown landing in the Pacific on July 24, 1969. But they couldn't just go back to their lives like nothing had happened. For 18 days, they were quarantined, just in case they'd picked up strange space germs that might be difficult to cure or cause a worldwide catastrophe.

In 1971, Neil Armstrong resigned from NASA. When Apollo 11 was over, he did everything he could to avoid being in public. Some say it's because he found the fame and attention overwhelming, while others say it's because he saw something on the moon. Either way, he decided to focus on teaching instead, serving as a professor of aerospace engineering at the University of Cincinnati, Ohio, from 1971 to 1979.

Afterward, Neil became the director or chairman for several companies, like AIL Systems (which made military-grade electronics) and Computing Technologies for Aviation. He was at the first company from 1977 until he retired in 2002, and the second from 1982 to 1992. He was involved with companies other than these two.

Neil also worked on the National Commission on Space, a panel that develops things for the space program to accomplish. He was also part of the Presidential Commission on the Space Shuttle Challenger Accident in 1986 to investigate what went wrong with the Challenger space shuttle that caused it to explode not too long after it launched, killing seven astronauts. In 2009, he received the Congressional Gold Medal.

Neil died in 2012 at 82 years old, but his first footprint is still on the moon, reminding every human on the planet that they can achieve the impossible if they put their minds to it. You can, too.

Famous Quotes

1. *There can be no great accomplishment without risk.*
2. *I believe every human has a finite number of heartbeats. I don't intend to waste any of mine.*
3. *You've got to expect things are going to go wrong. And we always need to prepare ourselves for handling the unexpected.*
4. *Each book holds an experience and an adventure.*
5. *Start at the end and work back.*

Bertrand Piccard

Bertrand Piccard was born in Lausanne, Switzerland, in 1958. He's an explorer, environmentalist, and psychiatrist. No wonder he loves to explore since he was born into a family tree of people like him. His grandfather, Auguste Piccard, was an explorer interested in the sea and the stratosphere. He was also a balloonist.

Bertrand Piccard.
COP PARIS, CC0, via Wikimedia Commons.
https://commons.wikimedia.org/wiki/File:Bertrand_Piccard_2015.jpg

Bertrand's father, Jacques, was an undersea explorer. You could say exploring is in their DNA. Auguste was the first person in the world to use a balloon to get to the stratosphere, while Jacques created and piloted a special craft he called bathyscaphes, which allowed him to explore the sea to his heart's content.

Piccard was exposed to aviation at a young age. At first, he was deathly afraid of heights, but he soon conquered this fear to go hang gliding when he was sixteen. He eventually became an excellent hang-gliding pilot. He loved everything about flying, so he explored other ways to be in the air, like piloting hot air balloons and ultralight planes.

Bertrand was fascinated by how humans act in extremely sticky or dangerous situations. He was so curious about the human mind that he studied psychiatry at the University of Lausanne, where he successfully completed his course with a degree. Later, he worked as a supervisor at the Swiss Medical Society for Hypnosis, SMSH. He lectured, too, but ballooning would always be his first love.

If there's one thing Bertrand didn't shy away from, it was challenging himself to do the impossible. He and Wim Verstraeten worked together for a while, hoping to travel around the world. The first time they tried was in 1997. Things might have worked out had it not been for the fuel leak in their craft. The cabin was filled with toxic fumes, making it impossible to keep going. The next time they tried was in 1998. They had their craft - Breitling Orbiter 2 - ready to go. It crashed in Myanmar in a rice paddy.

But Bertrand was no quitter. He gave it one more shot, this time with his copilot, Brian Jones. Before they went on this flight, other people had tried to beat them to it. Richard Branson and Steve Fossett gave it their best but failed. It seemed it was Bertrand's destiny to accomplish his goal before anyone else. Brian and Bertrand flew nonstop around the world in their balloon, the Breitling Orbiter 3.

The trip started on March 1, and it took them 19 days, 21 hours, and 55 minutes to finish on March 21. The explorers kicked off from the Swiss Alps and made their way through the skies of Europe, Africa, Asia, Central America, and the Pacific and Atlantic oceans. By law, they had to avoid no-fly zones. They also needed permission from China to fly undisturbed over the southern part of China, which was necessary because they needed the momentum of the jet stream airflow in that area to help them complete their mission. The flight ended with them touching down close to the Pyramids of Giza in Egypt.

Bertrand had done something so monumental that the Breitling Orbiter 3 gondola (the basket the balloon carries) is now displayed in Washington, D.C., at the Smithsonian Institution's National Air and Space Museum. In 2001, the French government gave him the Legion of Honor award. Now, Bertrand was famous. So, he did the smart thing by using his newfound fame to find ways to give back to people.

He turned his attention toward renewable energy, wondering if there was a way to create an aircraft powered by the sun that could cover thousands of miles as it traveled around the world without needing to land and refuel. In 2003, Piccard launched his Solar Impulse project with André Borschberg, a pilot and engineer from Switzerland. They had a plan: To create Bertrand's imagined solar-powered airplane.

The first plane was the Solar Impulse. André and Bertrand finished working on it in 2009. André flew the craft from July 7 to July 8, 2010, for a whopping 26 hours.

This was amazing because, for the first time, there was a solar-powered craft that could fly overnight. In 2011, they flew their plane from Payern, Switzerland, to Brussels, Belgium. That same year, they had another test flight from Brussels to Paris, and then in 2012, they flew 19 hours from Madrid, Spain, to Rabat, Morocco.

In 2011, Bertrand and his team began working on Solar Impulse 2. This time, they wanted a plane that could fly around the world. It took them three years to get it right, but they finally finished in 2014, once more, testing it first.

On March 9, 2015, André was airborne, taking off from Abu Dhabi to see if they'd created the best plane on the planet. Bertrand and André had to handle different legs on the flight. On July 3, André had to land in Kalaeloa, Hawaii. Unfortunately, the battery had gotten so hot on his trip from Japan that they had to pause their goal of traveling around the world.

Bertrand gave his Solar Impulse 2 one more shot on March 9, 2016. The takeoff on this attempt was also from Abu Dhabi. This time, the plane remained airborne for 118 hours, when it flew nonstop from Nagoya, Japan, to Kalaeloa, Hawaii. This is the longest solo flight that has ever been made. The plane finally finished its trip around Earth on July 26, when Bertrand piloted it back into Abu Dhabi and touched down.

It took a lot of work, planning, and failure along the way, but Bertrand Piccard proved that solar power is the future, and the future might as well start now. He forced the aviation industry (among others) to think beyond the limits of what they thought they could accomplish with clean technology.

Famous Quotes

1. *Adventure is something out of the usual pattern, a point at which you cannot avoid confronting the unknown so that you have to dig inside yourself to find the courage and resources to deal with what may lie ahead and to succeed.*
2. *Very often, human beings are living like on autopilot, reacting automatically with what happens. What interests me about the life of an explorer is you are in the unknown. You are out of your habits.*
3. *People put limitations on their creativity, believing they have to rely on what they know and what they have done.*

4. *Before achieving a dream, you need to make very little steps . . . People don't understand that when you want to make a big dream you have a lot of fastidious little things you have to do.*
5. *We know that dreams fuel innovation.*

Conclusion

You've made it to the end of this book, full of phenomenal stories to motivate and inspire you. Take the time to congratulate yourself for reading story after story until the end. If you really want this book to pay off, it's not enough to have read it to this point. You must stop and ask yourself what lessons you've learned. There's something to learn from every story if you pause for a bit and think about what resonates with you about each of these legendary people.

From one page to the next, you have seen what it means to persevere, why courage matters, and how to transform the world by being kind. You also know the power of determination. You've seen how you can turn even the worst failures into opportunities to succeed by focusing on what you want and refusing to settle for anything less.

You must have realized there's more to being successful than just winning if you've paid attention to the stories in this book. True success means growth. It's your willingness to learn all the time rather than think you know it all. It's about waking up each day with one plan: to be better than who you were yesterday. It's figuring out what matters to you, what you want to spend your life doing, and how to go after those dreams in good times and bad. Success is having the courage to dream of the impossible and then do all you can to make it possible and, eventually, real.

There will be times when you experience difficult situations. Sometimes, things won't work out how you want them to, and it feels like the whole world is trying to stop you from making your dreams happen.

In these times, remember these stories. Remember how these amazing people made the most magical things happen against all odds? Remember that, like them, you have a strength within you to tap into to overcome your challenges and obstacles. The only way to use this strength is to tell yourself, "I'm stronger than I think," and then go out there and prove it to yourself.

You, too, can be a hero. You don't need to wear fancy capes and suits, and you don't need superpowers like telepathy or laser eyes to make your dreams come true. Anyone who devotes themselves to their dreams is a hero. When you keep going after what you want, you're showing and teaching others it's okay for them to do the same. You're showing them they don't need to let their fears keep them from trying, failing, and trying again. You teach people that success isn't only about achieving the dream but enjoying the process.

Your life is your movie. What kind of hero do you want to be? How would you like to start? How do you see it ending, and what do you think you need to do to get there? Think about these things, and act on your dreams right away. One day, you, too, will have a story inspiring many because you dared to get started on your goals now. Believe in yourself, ignore those who doubt and discourage you from achieving your dreams, and you'll go a long way. You've got this.

If you enjoyed this book, I'd greatly appreciate a review on Amazon because it helps me to create more books that people want. It would mean a lot to hear from you.

To leave a review:

1. Open your camera app.
2. Point your mobile device at the QR code.
3. The review page will appear in your web browser.

Thanks for your support!

References

Albertson, S. (2017). The Biography of Princess Diana. Createspace Independent Publishing Platform.

Armstrong, N., Collins, M., Aldrin, E. E., Farmer, G., Hamblin, D. J., & Clarke, A. C. (2004). First on the Moon. A Voyage with Neil Armstrong, Michael Collins, and Edwin E. Aldrin, Jr. Little Brown & Co.

Biography.com, & Piccotti, T. (2021). Steve Jobs. Biography.com. https://www.biography.com/business-leaders/steve-jobs

Bolt, U. (2013). Faster than Lightning: My Autobiography. HarperCollins UK.

Bregel, S. (2024). Researchers say they may have just found Amelia Earhart's long-lost plane – experts aren't convinced. Www.bbc.com. https://www.bbc.com/future/article/20240131-researchers-say-amelia-earharts-long-lost-plane-may-have-just-been-found

Campbell, L. C. (2005). The Real Diana. Arcadia Books.

Clinton, C. (2008). Harriet Tubman The Road to Freedom. Paw Prints.

Deutsche Welle. (2024). Greta Thunberg on Trial in London for Defying Police. DW.com. https://www.dw.com/en/greta-thunberg-on-trial-in-london-for-defying-police/a-68140327

DuBois, H. (2022). Mother Teresa Facts, Biography, and Inspiration. Father Joe's Villages. https://my.neighbor.org/mother-teresa/

Einstein, A., & Swisher, C. (2002). Albert Einstein. Greenhaven Press.

European Commission. (2021). Italian Ambassador with a Determination Like No Other. Sport.ec.europa.eu. https://sport.ec.europa.eu/news/italian-ambassador-with-a-determination-like-no-other

Faccio, L. (2012). Messi: A Biography. Anchor Sports.

Geoff Blackwell. (2020). Greta Thunberg. Chronicle.

Haldy, E. E. (2016). Amelia Earhart. Cherry Lake Publishing.

Heather Moore Niver. (2016). Tim Berners-Lee: Inventor of the World Wide Web. Powerkids Press.

Hodges, A. (2012). Alan Turing: The Enigma. Princeton University Press, Princeton, New Jersey. (Original work published 1983)

Husain, Z. (2015). 9 Inspiring Malala Quotes. Unfoundation.org. https://unfoundation.org/blog/post/9-inspiring-malala-quotes/

Isaacson, W. (2017). Leonardo da Vinci. Simon and Schuster.

Isabel, M. (2020). David Attenborough. Frances Lincoln.

King, M. (2019). Good Neighbor: The Life and Work of Fred Rogers. Harry N. Abrams.

Lazenby, R. (2015). Michael Jordan: The Life. Back Bay Books, An Imprint Of Little, Brown And Company.

Lebreton, L., Egger, M., & Slat, B. (2020). Author Correction: A Global Mass Budget for Positively Buoyant Macroplastic Debris in the Ocean. Scientific Reports, 10(1). https://doi.org/10.1038/s41598-020-58755-4

Maddox, B. (2003). Rosalind Franklin: The Dark Lady of DNA. Harpercollins.

MarieCurie.org. (2016). Marie Curie the Scientist. Marie Curie. https://www.mariecurie.org.uk/who/our-history/marie-curie-the-scientist

Nguyen, V. A. (2019). 15 of Martin Luther King Jr.'s Most Inspiring Motivational Quotes. Parade; Parade. https://parade.com/252644/viannguyen/15-of-martin-luther-king-jr-s-most-inspiring-motivational-quotes/

Ofoego, O., & Muthoga, E. (2015). Wangari Maathai: and the Green Belt Movement. London Collins.

Piccard, B. (2009). A Trace in the Sky. White Star Publishers.

Schaefer, C. (2009). Frida Kahlo: A Biography. Greenwood Press.

Shay, D. (2024). Harriet Tubman. National Women's History Museum. https://www.womenshistory.org/education-resources/biographies/harriet-tubman

Singh, M. (2023). The Inspiring Success Story of Steve Jobs with 6 Life Lessons: Triumph and Transformation. Medium. https://medium.com/@hashtag_makhan/the-inspiring-success-story-of-steve-jobs-with-6-life-lessons-triumph-and-transformation-e003312dee9d

Socrates. (2013, January 12). Miracle Whiz Kid Jack Andraka: The Internet Is Not A Distraction. Singularity Weblog. https://www.singularityweblog.com/jack-andraka-on-singularity-1-on-1/

Stanley, D., & Hartland, J. (2016). Ada Lovelace, Poet of Science: The First Computer Programmer. Simon & Schuster Books For Young Readers.

The Fred Rogers Company. (2019). About Fred Rogers | Mister Rogers' Neighborhood. Mister Rogers' Neighborhood. https://www.misterrogers.org/about-fred-rogers/

The Nobel Prize. (2018). Martin Luther King Jr. Biographical. NobelPrize.org. https://www.nobelprize.org/prizes/peace/1964/king/biographical/

TIME USA, LLC. (2020). Meet TIME's First-Ever Kid of the Year. Time. https://time.com/5916772/kid-of-the-year-2020/

Vio, B. (2017). Mi Hanno Regalato un Sogno. La Scherma, Lo Spritz e le Paralimpiadi. Best Bureau.

Warner, J. (2016). MISTER ROGERS: A Biography of the Wonderful Life of Fred Rogers. CreateSpace Independent Publishing Platform.

Warren, M. (2018). Bones on remote Pacific island were likely Amelia Earhart's. Www.science.org. https://www.science.org/content/article/bones-remote-pacific-island-were-likely-amelia-earhart-s

White, M., & Gribbin, J. R. (2016). Stephen Hawking: A Life in Science. New York, NY Pegasus Books Llc.

Williams, S., & Paisner, D. (2010). My Life: Queen of the Court. Pocket

www.ingramcontent.com/pod-product-compliance
Lightning Source LLC
LaVergne TN
LVHW010627100826
845148LV00014B/3138
9798892961523